LIVE LIFE
Beautifully

366 days of ideas & inspiration

GOOD
HOUSEKEEPING

2024

PHASES OF THE MOON

● New moon   ◐ First quarter   ○ Full moon   ◑ Last quarter

This calendar is intended as a reference volume only, not as a medical manual. The information given here is designed to help you make informed decisions about your health. It is not intended as a substitute for any treatment that may have been prescribed by your doctor. If you suspect that you have a medical problem, we urge you to seek competent medical help.

Mention of specific companies, organizations, or authorities in this book does not imply endorsement by the author or publisher, nor does mention of specific companies, organizations, or authorities imply that they endorse this book, its author, or the publisher. Internet addresses and telephone numbers given in this book were accurate at the time it went to press.

Printed in China

Calendar design by Carol Angstadt
Photo editing by Monica Matthews
Photo credits can be found on the last page of the calendar.

ISBN 978-1-955710-18-3 hardcover
2 4 6 8 10 9 7 5 3 1 hardcover

HEARST

2023

SEPTEMBER
S	M	T	W	T	F	S
					1	2
3	4	5	6	7	8	9
10	11	12	13	14	15	16
17	18	19	20	21	22	23
24	25	26	27	28	29	30

OCTOBER
S	M	T	W	T	F	S
1	2	3	4	5	6	7
8	9	10	11	12	13	14
15	16	17	18	19	20	21
22	23	24	25	26	27	28
29	30	31				

NOVEMBER
S	M	T	W	T	F	S
			1	2	3	4
5	6	7	8	9	10	11
12	13	14	15	16	17	18
19	20	21	22	23	24	25
26	27	28	29	30		

DECEMBER
S	M	T	W	T	F	S
					1	2
3	4	5	6	7	8	9
10	11	12	13	14	15	16
17	18	19	20	21	22	23
24	25	26	27	28	29	30
31						

2024

JANUARY
S	M	T	W	T	F	S
	1	2	3	4	5	6
7	8	9	10	11	12	13
14	15	16	17	18	19	20
21	22	23	24	25	26	27
28	29	30	31			

FEBRUARY
S	M	T	W	T	F	S
				1	2	3
4	5	6	7	8	9	10
11	12	13	14	15	16	17
18	19	20	21	22	23	24
25	26	27	28	29		

MARCH
S	M	T	W	T	F	S
					1	2
3	4	5	6	7	8	9
10	11	12	13	14	15	16
17	18	19	20	21	22	23
24	25	26	27	28	29	30
31						

APRIL
S	M	T	W	T	F	S
	1	2	3	4	5	6
7	8	9	10	11	12	13
14	15	16	17	18	19	20
21	22	23	24	25	26	27
28	29	30				

MAY
S	M	T	W	T	F	S
			1	2	3	4
5	6	7	8	9	10	11
12	13	14	15	16	17	18
19	20	21	22	23	24	25
26	27	28	29	30	31	

JUNE
S	M	T	W	T	F	S
						1
2	3	4	5	6	7	8
9	10	11	12	13	14	15
16	17	18	19	20	21	22
23	24	25	26	27	28	29
30						

JULY
S	M	T	W	T	F	S
	1	2	3	4	5	6
7	8	9	10	11	12	13
14	15	16	17	18	19	20
21	22	23	24	25	26	27
28	29	30	31			

AUGUST
S	M	T	W	T	F	S
				1	2	3
4	5	6	7	8	9	10
11	12	13	14	15	16	17
18	19	20	21	22	23	24
25	26	27	28	29	30	31

SEPTEMBER
S	M	T	W	T	F	S
1	2	3	4	5	6	7
8	9	10	11	12	13	14
15	16	17	18	19	20	21
22	23	24	25	26	27	28
29	30					

OCTOBER
S	M	T	W	T	F	S
		1	2	3	4	5
6	7	8	9	10	11	12
13	14	15	16	17	18	19
20	21	22	23	24	25	26
27	28	29	30	31		

NOVEMBER
S	M	T	W	T	F	S
					1	2
3	4	5	6	7	8	9
10	11	12	13	14	15	16
17	18	19	20	21	22	23
24	25	26	27	28	29	30

DECEMBER
S	M	T	W	T	F	S
1	2	3	4	5	6	7
8	9	10	11	12	13	14
15	16	17	18	19	20	21
22	23	24	25	26	27	28
29	30	31				

2025

JANUARY
S	M	T	W	T	F	S
			1	2	3	4
5	6	7	8	9	10	11
12	13	14	15	16	17	18
19	20	21	22	23	24	25
26	27	28	29	30	31	

FEBRUARY
S	M	T	W	T	F	S
						1
2	3	4	5	6	7	8
9	10	11	12	13	14	15
16	17	18	19	20	21	22
23	24	25	26	27	28	

MARCH
S	M	T	W	T	F	S
						1
2	3	4	5	6	7	8
9	10	11	12	13	14	15
16	17	18	19	20	21	22
23	24	25	26	27	28	29
30	31					

APRIL
S	M	T	W	T	F	S
		1	2	3	4	5
6	7	8	9	10	11	12
13	14	15	16	17	18	19
20	21	22	23	24	25	26
27	28	29	30			

SEPTEMBER 2023

MONDAY	TUESDAY	WEDNESDAY	THURSDAY
4 Labor Day	5	6 ◑	7
11	12	13	14 ●
18	19	20	21
25	26	27	28

FRIDAY	SATURDAY	SUNDAY
1	2	3
8	9	10
15 Rosh Hashanah	16	17
22 ☽	23 First Day of Fall	24 Yom Kippur Begins
29 ○	30	

≋ **HOME HACK** ≋

Prove your progress. *Take before and after photos of your decluttering projects so you can see your accomplishments in vivid detail.*

AUGUST

M	T	W	T	F	S	S
	1	2	3	4	5	6
7	8	9	10	11	12	13
14	15	16	17	18	19	20
21	22	23	24	25	26	27
28	29	30	31			

OCTOBER

M	T	W	T	F	S	S
						1
2	3	4	5	6	7	8
9	10	11	12	13	14	15
16	17	18	19	20	21	22
23	24	25	26	27	28	29
30	31					

OCTOBER 2023

MONDAY	TUESDAY	WEDNESDAY	THURSDAY
2	3	4	5
9 Indigenous Peoples' Day	10	11	12
16	17	18	19
23	24	25	26
30	31 Halloween		

FRIDAY	SATURDAY	SUNDAY
		1
6	◐ 7	8
13	14	● 15
20	21	◑ 22
27	28	○ 29

≡ **KITCHEN HACK** ≡

Spray and save time. Soaking skillets in sudsy water can be time-consuming. Instead, spritz them with a dish spray to dissolve grease in minutes.

SEPTEMBER

M	T	W	T	F	S	S
				1	2	3
4	5	6	7	8	9	10
11	12	13	14	15	16	17
18	19	20	21	22	23	24
25	26	27	28	29	30	

NOVEMBER

M	T	W	T	F	S	S
		1	2	3	4	5
6	7	8	9	10	11	12
13	14	15	16	17	18	19
20	21	22	23	24	25	26
27	28	29	30			

NOVEMBER 2023

MONDAY	TUESDAY	WEDNESDAY	THURSDAY
		1 All Saints' Day	**2**
6	**7**	**8**	**9**
13 ●	**14**	**15**	**16**
20 ◐	**21**	**22**	**23** Thanksgiving
27 ○	**28**	**29**	**30**

FRIDAY	SATURDAY	SUNDAY
3	**4**	**5** Daylight Savings Time Ends ◗
10	**11** Veterans Day	**12** Diwali
17	**18**	**19**
24	**25**	**26**

notes

⚡ **LIFE HACK** ⚡

Make a mantra. Contemplating a big change? Reflect on your upcoming goals and come up with a phrase that helps you focus on what matters most.

OCTOBER

M	T	W	T	F	S	S
						1
2	3	4	5	6	7	8
9	10	11	12	13	14	15
16	17	18	19	20	21	22
23	24	25	26	27	28	29
30	31					

DECEMBER

M	T	W	T	F	S	S
				1	2	3
4	5	6	7	8	9	10
11	12	13	14	15	16	17
18	19	20	21	22	23	24
25	26	27	28	29	30	31

DECEMBER 2023

MONDAY	TUESDAY	WEDNESDAY	THURSDAY
4	5 ◐	6	7 Hanukkah Begins
11	12 ●	13	14
18	19 ◑	20	21 First Day of Winter
25 Christmas Day	26 First Day of Kwanzaa ○	27	28

FRIDAY	SATURDAY	SUNDAY
1	**2**	**3** First Day of Advent
8	**9**	**10**
15	**16**	**17**
22	**23**	**24** Christmas Eve
29	**30**	**31** New Year's Eve

notes

NOVEMBER

M	T	W	T	F	S	S
		1	2	3	4	5
6	7	8	9	10	11	12
13	14	15	16	17	18	19
20	21	22	23	24	25	26
27	28	29	30			

JANUARY

M	T	W	T	F	S	S
1	2	3	4	5	6	7
8	9	10	11	12	13	14
15	16	17	18	19	20	21
22	23	24	25	26	27	28
29	30	31				

Make every day
EXTRAORDINARY

Your goal in 2024: Look for new ways to live your best life and enjoy memorable moments every day. Use these handy checklists to plan how to prioritize—and then celebrate—what matters most to you.

★

CHECKLIST

DAILY

renew
- ◯ Journal for five minutes
- ◯ Take a catnap
- ◯ _____
- ◯ _____

refresh
- ◯ Swing your arms when walking
- ◯ Open a window— even in winter
- ◯ _____
- ◯ _____

remember
- ◯ Use sunscreen
- ◯ Plan tomorrow's menu
- ◯ _____
- ◯ _____

rejoice
- ◯ Seek beauty—stop and smell the flowers
- ◯ Make a gratitude list
- ◯ _____
- ◯ _____

other
- ◯ _____
- ◯ _____

★

CHECKLIST

WEEKLY

renew
- ○ Take a long soak in the bath
- ○ Make time to read
- ○ _____
- ○ _____

refresh
- ○ Tidy up a problem space
- ○ Vacuum the house
- ○ _____
- ○ _____

remember
- ○ Check inbox for important messages
- ○ Plan outfits for the coming week
- ○ _____
- ○ _____

rejoice
- ○ Try a new veggie dish
- ○ Call a friend just to say hi
- ○ _____
- ○ _____

other
- ○ _____
- ○ _____

MONTHLY

renew

- ☐ Give a spontaneous gift
- ☐ Watch a comedy show
- ☐ _____
- ☐ _____

refresh

- ☐ Clean out your handbag
- ☐ Vacuum furniture
- ☐ _____
- ☐ _____

remember

- ☐ Plan a weekend day trip
- ☐ Set a fitness goal
- ☐ _____
- ☐ _____

rejoice

- ☐ Call in a favor
- ☐ Visit an older relative you haven't seen in awhile
- ☐ _____
- ☐ _____

other

- ☐ _____
- ☐ _____

CHECKLIST

WINTER

renew
○ Use a hydrating facial mask
○ Take an online class
○ _____
○ _____

refresh
○ Launder sweaters
○ Donate old coats
○ _____
○ _____

remember
○ Stock up on gift-wrapping
○ Check smoke alarms
○ _____
○ _____

rejoice
○ Watch a favorite holiday movie
○ Try a new dessert recipe
○ _____
○ _____

other
○ _____
○ _____

SPRING

renew
- ○ Buy a new pair of rain boots
- ○ Get a pedicure
- ○ _____
- ○ _____

refresh
- ○ Tackle a new garden project
- ○ Reorganize a closet
- ○ _____
- ○ _____

remember
- ○ Plan a potluck with friends
- ○ Flip mattresses
- ○ _____
- ○ _____

rejoice
- ○ Attend a concert
- ○ Seek out a garden show
- ○ _____
- ○ _____

other
- ○ _____
- ○ _____

CHECKLIST

SUMMER

renew
- ○ Take a nature walk
- ○ Swing in a hammock
- ○ _____
- ○ _____

refresh
- ○ Hang patio lights
- ○ Hold a garage sale
- ○ _____
- ○ _____

remember
- ○ Restock first aid kit
- ○ Change guest room linens
- ○ _____
- ○ _____

rejoice
- ○ Plan a beach day
- ○ Say YES to a spontaneous invitation
- ○ _____
- ○ _____

other
- ○ _____
- ○ _____

GOLDFINCH

FALL

renew

- ○ Wear a cozy sweater
- ○ Simmer cinnamon on the stove
- ○ _____
- ○ _____

refresh

- ○ Plant spring bulbs
- ○ Create a seasonal centerpiece
- ○ _____
- ○ _____

remember

- ○ Review gift-giving budget
- ○ Plan, make, and freeze casseroles
- ○ _____
- ○ _____

rejoice

- ○ Go on a hayride
- ○ Frame a favorite photograph
- ○ _____
- ○ _____

other

- ○ _____
- ○ _____

Your Guide to a Refreshing
WINTER

Looking to renew and recharge this season? Here you'll find plenty of inspiring ways to make little changes with real impact on the days ahead.

FEEL CALMER
Now

To inspire a sense of peace in a chaotic world, focus on what you can control—your state of mind and your surroundings. These tweaks can help:

CANCEL SOMETHING. Look at your calendar and find one thing you really, truly don't have to attend, like a meeting that can go on just fine without you or a social event you're not feeling psyched about. Bow out and replace it with . . . nothing. "You know your body needs sleep, but it also needs rest, and those are two different things," says Asha Tarry, L.M.S.W., a psychotherapist and the author of *Adulting as a Millennial.* Giving yourself permission to do nothing will recharge your battery, lower your blood pressure and allow you to think more clearly, she adds.

DECLUTTER YOUR FRIDGE DOOR. The room where your family gathers to cook, eat and laugh should be a calming oasis—but it won't be if the refrigerator is covered with paperwork, bills, menus and coupons. Spend a few minutes each week purging, suggests GH Home Editor Monique Valeris. "Get rid of dated paperwork, old photos and broken magnets—and toss the takeout menus, since you can get that info online," she says. Instead of having a messy mix of flyers and invites, write down every important date on a magnetic dry-erase calendar.

HANG ART

Even though hanging art is a task that often takes just a few minutes of your time, it's a task that almost everyone puts off for longer than they should. "Almost every one of my virtual clients has a piece of wall art that has been leaning against the wall waiting to be hung for far too long," shares expert organizer and *Keep This Toss That* author Jamie Novak. If you have a poster or photo you've been meaning to hang for ages now, then today's the day to finally get it hung. It's such an easy way to make your space feel complete.

Before hanging your picture, make sure you gather your hanging hardware, figure out your ideal hanging height and make sure you have a level handy. And if you're looking to upgrade a blank wall space and don't have any art to hang, visit goodhousekeeping.com for some DIY wall decor ideas.

DEEP CONDITION WHILE YOU SLEEP

What's the key to keeping your tresses healthy?
Moisturize, moisturize, moisturize—which will also help prevent split ends, frizz and breakage. If your regular conditioner isn't cutting it, opt for an intensive overnight treatment with coconut oil, says Kyle White, a colorist at Oscar Blandi Salon in NYC.

MOISTURE TREATMENT:
1 Tbsp coconut oil

HOW-TO BEFORE BED: Warm coconut oil in the microwave, then massage it into damp hair, avoiding the roots. (Tie strands in a bun and/or cover with a shower cap or a hair wrap if desired.) Shampoo in the morning.

CREATE A "TODAY" LIST

Stacking your day with too many tasks can make it harder to concentrate—and the more frazzled you feel, the more likely you are to reach for high-sugar, high-fat foods. "People add their entire life's goals to their to-do list and end up feeling overwhelmed," says registered dietitian Daniela Neman. Instead, write down five things you want to get done each day. You'll feel more in control of your work—and your cravings.

PUSH BACK DINNERTIME

Late-night snacking is the worst kind, and research from Brigham Young University may explain why: Brain scans show that we simply don't get the same high from food eaten later in the evening as we do from food eaten earlier. In other words, food we eat later feels less rewarding, and that can lead to overeating.

"If you normally have dinner around 6 p.m., try eating a healthy snack then and serving dinner a little later, around 8 p.m.," says Stacy T. Sims, Ph.D., founder of Osmo Nutrition. By the time you clean up and watch a little TV, you'll be ready to hit the sack, not the fridge.

RECIPE OF THE SEASON!

Make a Relaxing Meal

ROASTED TOMATO SOUP

Active **20 min.** | Total **45 min.**

Soup is the perfect anti-stress meal. This one has rich swirls of sour cream that create a tangy flavor contrast and make the finished dish look impressive.

2½ lbs tomatoes, halved
3 Tbsp olive oil
Kosher salt
Pepper
1 large red onion, chopped
4 cloves garlic, chopped
2 jalapeños (seeded, if desired), chopped
4 cups vegetable broth
Sour cream

1. Heat oven to 400°F. On a rimmed baking sheet, toss tomatoes with 1 Tbsp oil and ¼ tsp each salt and pepper. Roast until very tender and lightly browned, 20 to 25 min.
2. Meanwhile, heat remaining 2 Tbsp oil in a large Dutch oven or pot over medium heat. Add onion, season with ½ tsp each salt and pepper, and cook, covered, stirring occasionally until very tender, 10 to 12 min. Stir in garlic and jalapeños and cook for 2 min.
3. Transfer tomatoes and any pan juices to the pot. Add broth and bring to a boil. Reduce heat and simmer for 10 min. Using an immersion blender (or a standard blender, working in batches), purée soup. Top with a swirl of sour cream, if desired.

SERVES 4 About 180 cal, 11 g fat (2 g sat fat), 3 g pro, 705 mg sodium, 21 g carb, 4 g fiber

JANUARY 2024

MONDAY	TUESDAY	WEDNESDAY	THURSDAY
1 New Year's Day	**2**	**3** ◑	**4**
8	**9**	**10**	**11** ●
15 Martin Luther King Jr. Day	**16**	**17** ◐	**18**
22	**23**	**24**	**25** ○
29	**30**	**31**	

FRIDAY	SATURDAY	SUNDAY
5	**6**	**7**
12	**13**	**14**
19	**20**	**21**
26	**27**	**28**

BUILD BETTER BOUNDARIES

Healthy boundaries are rooted in self-love and have a significant impact on our overall happiness. If you feel exhausted, over-extended, or as if you're doing too much for others at the expense of yourself, **it might be time to reconsider your habits**. "Boundaries establish healthy relationships and a sense of identity," says Brian Wind, Ph.D., chief clinical officer at Journey Pure addiction centers. "They boost your self-esteem and reduce resentment and anger."

DECEMBER

M	T	W	T	F	S	S
				1	2	3
4	5	6	7	8	9	10
11	12	13	14	15	16	17
18	19	20	21	22	23	24
25	26	27	28	29	30	31

FEBRUARY

M	T	W	T	F	S	S
			1	2	3	4
5	6	7	8	9	10	11
12	13	14	15	16	17	18
19	20	21	22	23	24	25
26	27	28	29			

JANUARY 1–7

2024

M	T	W	T	F	S	S
1	2	3	4	5	6	7
8	9	10	11	12	13	14
15	16	17	18	19	20	21
22	23	24	25	26	27	28
29	30	31				

"Seasons change, and so do we."

—NIKKICHE

1 MONDAY New Year's Day

2 TUESDAY

3 WEDNESDAY ◑

4 THURSDAY

5 FRIDAY

6 SATURDAY

7 SUNDAY

JANUARY 8-14
2024

M	T	W	T	F	S	S
1	2	3	4	5	6	7
8	**9**	**10**	**11**	**12**	**13**	**14**
15	16	17	18	19	20	21
22	23	24	25	26	27	28
29	30	31				

Find Serenity in Solitude

Getting away from the external world to be alone with your thoughts and find a sense of calm is a great way to disconnect from distractions and look inward for happiness. We're wired to connect with others, so finding solitude might seem difficult at first. But it's necessary — a study performed at the University of California, Santa Cruz, revealed that solitude is a "biological need" and that it "supports identity development as well as intimacy with others" and "promotes happiness." Try looking at solitude as a way to recharge your mind and reconnect with your values to allow better connection with others. Work to develop a daily practice by spending some time alone every day, noticing your thoughts and directing them toward "the greatest ideal of yourself," says Joe Dispenza, Ph.D., a personal-transformation teacher featured in the film *What the Bleep Do We Know!?*

8 MONDAY

9 TUESDAY

10 WEDNESDAY

11 THURSDAY ●

12 FRIDAY

13 SATURDAY

14 SUNDAY

JANUARY 15-21
2024

M	T	W	T	F	S	S
1	2	3	4	5	6	7
8	9	10	11	12	13	14
15	16	17	18	19	20	21
22	23	24	25	26	27	28
29	30	31				

Maximize Prep and Recovery Time

While fitness starts with exercise, the post-workout rest period is what creates the results. "Muscles grow and get stronger as they adapt to the stimulus you subjected them to during those intense workouts," says Tony Maloney, an ACSM-certified trainer and head coach at Orangetheory Fitness in Noblesville, IN. His rule of thumb is 1 to 2: That is, after an intense training session, give your body two full days to recover.

Another way to keep muscles in peak condition? Consider adding a foam roller to your routine. A light dynamic stretch before and after working out will keep muscles from getting tight. If you don't have a roller, try a peanut ball, which you can make by taping two tennis balls together—perfect for digging into muscles around the neck and spine.

15 MONDAY Martin Luther King Jr. Day

16 TUESDAY

17 WEDNESDAY ◐

18 THURSDAY

19 FRIDAY

20 SATURDAY

21 SUNDAY

JANUARY 22-28

2024

M	T	W	T	F	S	S
1	2	3	4	5	6	7
8	9	10	11	12	13	14
15	16	17	18	19	20	21
22	23	24	25	26	27	28
29	30	31				

Consider Intuitive Eating

"A lot of people think there's an all or nothing way of eating," explains Alissa Rumsey, R.D., a certified intuitive eating counselor and author of *Unapologetic Eating.* "I know of so many people who won't do things because of their bodies. They'll say, 'When I lose the weight, then I'll start dating or go on vacation or get my master's degree!'" Imagine if you decided to go ahead and just do those things, no matter what the numbers on the scale said.

Eating food that makes you feel nourished and that you enjoy— without counting the number of calories or carbs—may in fact be the key to remaining at a steady weight, stabilizing both your emotions and your health. "When people shift behaviors around food and eating and movement and stress management and sleep, even when their weight stays exactly the same, we see a decrease in the disease risk and an improvement in health," says Rumsey. "Intuitive eating is about taking care of your body rather than trying to punish or control it."

22 MONDAY

23 TUESDAY

24 WEDNESDAY

25 THURSDAY ○

26 FRIDAY

27 SATURDAY

28 SUNDAY

FEBRUARY 2024

MONDAY	TUESDAY	WEDNESDAY	THURSDAY
			1
5	6	7	8
12 Lincoln's Birthday	13	14 Valentine's Day	15
19 Presidents' Day	20	21	22
26	27	28	29

FRIDAY	SATURDAY	SUNDAY
2 Groundhog Day ◐	**3**	**4**
9 ●	**10** Chinese New Year	**11**
16 ◑	**17**	**18**
23	**24** ○	**25**

Feel Good Goal

LEARN ABOUT YOURSELF

If you've lost touch with who you are—who you really are—over the years because you've been so busy being of service to others, it's time to get that back. "Developing a loving relationship with yourself brings an inward sense of peace and fulfillment," says Sheenie Ambardar, MD, a clinical psychiatrist and psychotherapist who specializes in happiness. **Write down a list of what makes you _you_, including things that you like about yourself.**

JANUARY

M	T	W	T	F	S	S
1	2	3	4	5	6	7
8	9	10	11	12	13	14
15	16	17	18	19	20	21
22	23	24	25	26	27	28
29	30	31				

MARCH

M	T	W	T	F	S	S
				1	2	3
4	5	6	7	8	9	10
11	12	13	14	15	16	17
18	19	20	21	22	23	24
25	26	27	28	29	30	31

JANUARY 29– FEBRUARY 4

2024

M	T	W	T	F	S	S
29	30	31	1	2	3	4
5	6	7	8	9	10	11
12	13	14	15	16	17	18
19	20	21	22	23	24	25
26	27	28	29			

"Love is the flower you've got to let grow."

—JOHN LENNON

29 MONDAY

30 TUESDAY

31 WEDNESDAY

1 THURSDAY

2 FRIDAY Groundhog Day ◑

3 SATURDAY

4 SUNDAY

FEBRUARY 5–11
2024

M	T	W	T	F	S	S
			1	2	3	4
5	6	7	8	9	10	11
12	13	14	15	16	17	18
19	20	21	22	23	24	25
26	27	28	29			

Quit Sabotaging Your Sleep

If you start another episode of your most recent Netflix binge at 1 a.m. with a hectic morning to come, you're engaging in what sleep experts call "revenge bedtime procrastination." Sound familiar? Try these techniques:

1. **Rethink your schedule.** Your late-night habits may be fueled by not having enough free time. Take a hard look at your day to work in "me time" long before bed.

2. **Turn off autoplay.** Letting go of TV in bed is hard to do, but disabling the autoplay function on Netflix or Hulu can help.

3. **Block yourself.** A browser extension (such as RescueTime) or an app (like Freedom) can physically kick you off social media feeds or lock you out of your inbox at a certain time.

TRY THIS TO FEEL
CALM

Zap allergens. For a relaxing night's sleep without the sniffles: Steam, then vacuum pillows and plush toys to remove dust, pollen and germs.

5 MONDAY

6 TUESDAY

7 WEDNESDAY

8 THURSDAY

9 FRIDAY ●

10 SATURDAY Chinese New Year

11 SUNDAY

FEBRUARY 12-18
2024

M	T	W	T	F	S	S
			1	2	3	4
5	6	7	8	9	10	11
12	13	14	15	16	17	18
19	20	21	22	23	24	25
26	27	28	29			

Make a Batch of Pancakes

Heart-shaped pancakes are a simple way to get everyone in the Valentine spirit first thing in the morning. To make them, pour your favorite pancake batter into a heart-shaped cookie cutter and remove the cookie cutter before you flip. You can also draw a freehand heart by putting your batter in a pastry bag for precision. Top with your favorite berries for a bright pop of color and flavor.

As for the secret to perfectly fluffy pancakes, it's simple: Don't overmix the dry and wet ingredients. Give it a few whisks, just until all the flour is moistened. There's no need to mix the batter until all lumps are gone because they'll dissolve naturally.

TRY THIS TO FEEL
HAPPY

Laugh with loved ones.
Researchers have found that social laughter releases endorphins (a.k.a. feel-good hormones) in our brains. Not only will you benefit from the giggles, but laughing can strengthen your relationships!

12 MONDAY Lincoln's Birthday

13 TUESDAY

14 WEDNESDAY Valentine's Day

15 THURSDAY

16 FRIDAY ◑

17 SATURDAY

18 SUNDAY

FEBRUARY 19-25
2024

M	T	W	T	F	S	S
			1	2	3	4
5	6	7	8	9	10	11
12	13	14	15	16	17	18
19	**20**	**21**	**22**	**23**	**24**	**25**
26	27	28	29			

Quit Overthinking

Overthinking can lead to hours of agonizing over mundane things. Instead, use these tips to proactively leave those thoughts behind:

1. **Do a reality check.** Acknowledge when you're obsessing about something and ask yourself: Can it be changed? Is this a problem that needs to be solved right now? If not, try to set the issue aside for the moment.

2. **Distract yourself.** Watch a movie or play a game. We can't focus well on two things at once, so keeping our brains busy helps us stop ruminating.

3. **Set a timer.** Allow five minutes to edit an email instead of tweaking it for 30.

4. **Recognize when a pro could help.** Self-help may not be enough if your overthinking is part of clinical depression or anxiety.

TRY THIS TO FEEL
HAPPY

Reframe your thinking. Rather than approach tasks with "I have to do XYZ," just say "I get to do XYZ." This subtle shift can pave the way for a whole new perspective to emerge.

19 MONDAY Presidents' Day

20 TUESDAY

21 WEDNESDAY

22 THURSDAY

23 FRIDAY

24 SATURDAY ○

25 SUNDAY

MARCH 2024

MONDAY	TUESDAY	WEDNESDAY	THURSDAY
4	**5**	**6**	**7**
11 Ramadan Begins	**12**	**13**	**14** Pi Day
18	**19** First Day of Spring	**20**	**21**
25 Holi Begins ○	**26**	**27**	**28**

FRIDAY	SATURDAY	SUNDAY	
1	2	3	◗
8	9	10 Daylight Savings Time Begins ●	
15	16	17 St. Patrick's Day ◑	
22	23	24 Palm Sunday	
29	30	31 Easter Sunday	

Feel Good Goal

LIVE IN LAUGHTER

When we laugh, the brain releases happy hormones that lower inflammation, boost cardiovascular health, relax your muscles, and improve concentration. As an antidote to the negative effects of stress, laughter is key to well-being. **Make a habit out of looking for laughter**: You can take time to find funny videos, watch a favorite sitcom, or even keep a list on your phone of things you find funny throughout the day to share with someone later on.

FEBRUARY

M	T	W	T	F	S	S
			1	2	3	4
5	6	7	8	9	10	11
12	13	14	15	16	17	18
19	20	21	22	23	24	25
26	27	28	29			

APRIL

M	T	W	T	F	S	S
1	2	3	4	5	6	7
8	9	10	11	12	13	14
15	16	17	18	19	20	21
22	23	24	25	26	27	28
29	30					

M	T	W	T	F	S	S
26	27	28	29	1	2	3
4	5	6	7	8	9	10
11	12	13	14	15	16	17
18	19	20	21	22	23	24
25	26	27	28	29	30	31

"Self-care is how you take your power back."

—LALAH DELIA

26 MONDAY

27 TUESDAY

28 WEDNESDAY

29 THURSDAY

1 FRIDAY

2 SATURDAY

3 SUNDAY ☽

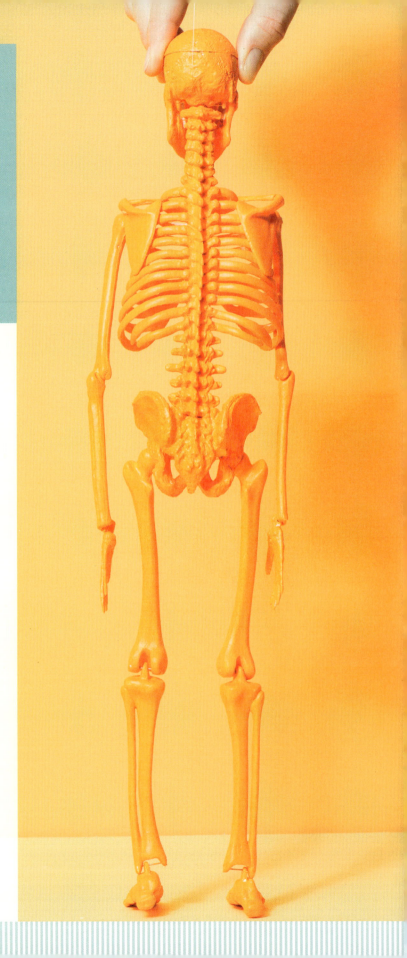

MARCH 4–10
2024

M	T	W	T	F	S	S
				1	2	3
4	**5**	**6**	**7**	**8**	**9**	**10**
11	12	13	14	15	16	17
18	19	20	21	22	23	24
25	26	27	28	29	30	31

Exercise for a Stronger Skeleton

Weight-bearing movements push bone-building cells into action and strengthen bones. Consider trying one of these quick exercises.

IF YOU'RE NOT INTO TRADITIONAL CARDIO... Try what's called 5-10-15 training, in which you alternate high-speed, moderate-paced and slower running for that number of seconds, respectively, then repeat the cycle several times. Doing this three times a week increases levels of a protein involved in bone construction and boosts bone mineral density in less than two months, Danish researchers discovered.

OR JUST TAKE A FLYING LEAP... Stand up. Jump off the ground. Land. Wait 30 seconds (to prevent bone from becoming desensitized). Repeat 20 times. When 60 premenopausal women did this twice a day for four months, their hip bone mineral density improved significantly, according to researchers at Brigham Young University. Can't manage 20? Even doing 10 leaps twice daily has benefits.

4 MONDAY

5 TUESDAY

6 WEDNESDAY

7 THURSDAY

8 FRIDAY

9 SATURDAY

10 SUNDAY ● Daylight Savings Time Begins

MARCH 11-17

2024

M	T	W	T	F	S	S
				1	2	3
4	5	6	7	8	9	10
11	12	13	14	15	16	17
18	19	20	21	22	23	24
25	26	27	28	29	30	31

Quick & Delicious Dip Combos

A good dip makes vitamin and mineral-filled vegetables a treat, says Dawn Jackson Blatner, R.D.N., author of *The Superfood Swap*. Dig into her quick and tasty options.

Plain Greek yogurt + dill + feta
DIPPERS: Cucumbers and cherry tomatoes

Tahini + everything bagel seasoning
DIPPER: Bell peppers

Peanut butter + rice vinegar + cayenne pepper (optional)
DIPPER: Broccoli florets

Mashed avocado + lime + salt + pepper
DIPPERS: Jicama and pepper strips

TRY THIS TO FEEL
CALM

Set aside time in the morning before a party to wash and prep all your vegetables. It will make those last few minutes before guests arrive so much more relaxing.

11 MONDAY Ramadan Begins

12 TUESDAY

13 WEDNESDAY

14 THURSDAY Pi Day

15 FRIDAY

16 SATURDAY

17 SUNDAY ◑ St. Patrick's Day

MARCH 18-24

2024

M	T	W	T	F	S	S
				1	2	3
4	5	6	7	8	9	10
11	12	13	14	15	16	17
18	**19**	**20**	**21**	**22**	**23**	**24**
25	26	27	28	29	30	31

Restore Calm with Counting

The 5-4-3-2-1 rule is a mindfulness strategy that is all about engaging your five senses to bring you out of your anxious ruminations and ground you in the present. "Look around the room and name five things you can see, four things you can feel, three things you can hear, two things you can smell and one thing you can taste," says Michele Goldman, Psy.D., a clinical psychologist and a media advisory group member for the Hope for Depression Research Foundation.

This simple exercise creates a pause in your thinking pattern that can help you become aware of your immediate surroundings versus whatever is distracting you in your head. If you're by yourself, try naming the things you notice out loud to really remind yourself that nothing alarming is happening now.

18 MONDAY

19 TUESDAY First Day of Spring

20 WEDNESDAY

21 THURSDAY

22 FRIDAY

23 SATURDAY

24 SUNDAY Palm Sunday

MARCH 25–31
2024

M	T	W	T	F	S	S
				1	2	3
4	5	6	7	8	9	10
11	12	13	14	15	16	17
18	19	20	21	22	23	24
25	26	27	28	29	30	31

Create a Simply Stunning Coffee Nook

Turn a small, underutilized space into the ultimate caffeination station. Interior designer Ashley Gilbreath converted a closet into a stylish coffee bar complete with built-in shelves to store mugs, stirrers and other essentials.

Hide machines and cords behind a curtain, then peel it back when it's time to brew your cup. Unexpected accents like faux palms, whimsical wallpaper and a chic pendant light elevate the design. "It's important to make sure colors and patterns don't overpower a space, and in this instance the wallpaper print attracts attention, but doesn't scream at you," she says.

TRY THIS TO FEEL
CALM

Indulge in a fancy coffee at home. Bring the relaxing vibes of your local café to your kitchen by turning your boring cup of joe into a cozy cappuccino with steamed milk.

25 MONDAY ○ Holi Begins

26 TUESDAY

27 WEDNESDAY

28 THURSDAY

29 FRIDAY

30 SATURDAY

31 SUNDAY Easter Sunday

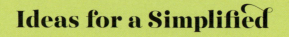

Ideas for a Simplified
SPRING

Get a head start on a few of those projects you've had on your to-do list and enjoy feeling ready to relax in a well-organized space.

Enlarge a Small Space

THINK IN SECTIONS. Divide a room geometrically into quarters, thirds or halves, then assign each section a function—like sleeping or eating—and design around that function.

PICK LIGHTER COLORS FOR WALLS AND FLOORS. Lighter tones give the illusion of more space.

CHOOSE FURNITURE THAT DOES DOUBLE DUTY. A daybed tucked into a reading nook works equally well for lazy Sundays and houseguests.

GO FULL SIZE. Select a few full-size furniture pieces instead of cramming in lots of smaller ones. The room will feel more expansive.

LEAVE SOME OPENNESS. Resist the urge to cram a small space with tons of stuff.

SET THINGS BACK. Recessed shelving gives depth to tight quarters.

Decluttering 101

Oftentimes, the hardest part about minimizing the clutter in your home is knowing where to start. One thing that's clear, though, is that it's overwhelming to try to tackle an entire house at once—which is why you should focus on one room at a time.

Another good approach is to start with the visible areas first—so things like shelves, furniture and objects on the floor—before moving onto the hidden areas in the room, like organiz-

> 1. DO I NEED IT?
>
> 2. DO I USE IT?
>
> 3. WHAT WOULD I USE IF I DIDN'T HAVE IT?
>
> 4. WHY DO I HAVE IT?

ing your drawers, cabinets and the closet. This way, you'll be able to actually see your progress as you go along, says Joshua Becker, writer of the *Becoming Minimalist* blog and author of *The Minimalist Home: A Room-by-Room Guide to a Decluttered, Refocused Life.*

If you're still having trouble deciding to keep or toss something, Becker recommends four specific questions (left) to ask yourself about the particular item.

HIDE THINGS IN PLAIN SIGHT

Don't let design challenges like radiators or thermostats get in the way of your aesthetic. Try these creative hacks and DIYs to blend style and function seamlessly.

HIDE A THERMOSTAT BEHIND WALL ART. This gallery wall isn't just a form of expression for self-taught DIYer Cass Smith. The middle of the arrangement features a piece of art that can be opened to reveal (and closed to hide) a clunky thermostat. "Since the wall space was so awkward and empty, this irregular gallery wall does a perfect job of filling the space and also creates lots of character," Smith says. All it took to do the trick was a

vintage frame, two pieces of wood, hinges, screws and a magnetic catch.

COVER A RADIATOR WITH A STYLISH SHELF. It's never easy to make a radiator in a historic home look good. But Lauren Macke of Home Theology, a design blog and interior design firm, pulled it off in her 105-year-old Bluffton, OH, home with a DIY cane radiator cover. "The natural cane allows heat to easily escape and warm the room, while the faux doors and brass hardware give the look of a pretty piece of furniture," she says of the entryway space.

MASTER THE ART OF HANDWASHING

Give special sweaters, lingerie and delicates a little TLC. Here's how:

1 Mix up sudsy water. Add detergent to the sink or basin as the water is running so it dissolves completely. Give the solution a quick stir to be sure it is fully mixed.

2 Gently place your garment in the suds. Immerse your garment. Submerge your clothing item, gently squeezing the suds through the fabric.

3 Let it soak for five to 10 minutes, turn it over and squeeze again. Soak for five to 10 minutes more.

4 Rinse thoroughly. Carefully remove the wet garment and drain the sink. Fill with cool water, lay your item in it and swish to rinse.

5 Squeeze out—don't wring out—excess water. Roll in a towel.

6 Lay flat to dry. Place the garment flat on a dry towel or a mesh rack, blocking it back into shape. When the top is dry, flip it over to give the back more air. Swap in a dry towel if needed.

CRACK THE CLEAN CODE

Look for garment care labels in the side seam, back neck or back waist of clothing.

HOW TO WASH

MACHINE WASH	HAND WASH	NEVER WASH	NORMAL TEMP	COLD TEMP	WARM TEMP
HOT TEMP	BLEACH WHEN NEEDED	NON-CHLORINE BLEACH	DO NOT BLEACH	DO NOT DRY CLEAN	DRY CLEAN ONLY

HOW TO DRY

NORMAL HEAT	LOW HEAT	MEDIUM HEAT	HIGH HEAT	NO HEAT	TUMBLE DRY
NEVER DRY	LINE DRY	DRIP DRY	RESHAPE AND LAY FLAT TO DRY	DRY IN SHADE	DO NOT WRING

HOW TO IRON

ANY TEMP	LOW TEMP	MEDIUM TEMP	HIGH TEMP	DO NOT STEAM	DO NOT IRON

Make This Tonight!

CALIFORNIA ROLL SALAD

Active **15 min.** | Total **15 min.**

We "unrolled" the components of this Japanese dish and added a drizzle of spicy mayo. Top it off with furikake, a seasoning combo of sesame seeds and dried seaweed, available at most supermarkets.

- 2 Tbsp mayonnaise
- 1 Tbsp sriracha
- 1 Tbsp fresh lemon juice
  Kosher salt
- 1 to 2 heads Boston lettuce, separated into leaves
- 1½ cups cooked short-grain brown rice
- 2 Persian cucumbers, thinly sliced into ribbons
- 1 avocado, cut into pieces
- 8 oz surimi or crabmeat
- 1 scallion, thinly sliced
  Furikake seasoning, for sprinkling

1. In small bowl, whisk together mayonnaise, sriracha, lemon juice and a pinch of salt.
2. Among bowls, divide lettuce, rice, cucumber and avocado. Top with surimi, then drizzle with dressing. Sprinkle with scallion and furikake if desired.

SERVES 4 About 280 cal, 13.5 g fat (2 g sat), 10 g pro, 595 mg sodium, 33 g carb, 6 g fiber

SALAD 101

Spring is the perfect time of year to reboot your lunch routine with a healthy salad that is truly satisfying and delicious. So what are the healthiest salads? You can choose a wide variety of veggies—the more colorful the better—to help ensure that you get an array of nutrients, and look for ones that are high in fiber, which will keep you feeling satisfied.

Use creamy dressings sparingly, and make judicious use of cheese: Pick more flavorful types, like feta or Parm, that will pack a punch even in small amounts. Instead of croutons, try a handful of sunflower seeds or pepitas. Herbs are perfect for adding flavor without any fat, but make sure to give 'em a wash and dry (it's easy with a pick from our best salad spinners), especially if they're a little sandy.

For plenty of ideas and inspiration, check out our recipes on **goodhousekeeping.com.**

APRIL 2024

MONDAY	TUESDAY	WEDNESDAY	THURSDAY
1 April Fools' Day ◑	**2**	**3**	**4**
8 ●	**9**	**10** Eid al-Fitr	**11**
15 Tax Day ◐	**16**	**17**	**18**
22 Passover Begins Earth Day	**23** ○	**24**	**25**
29	**30**		

FRIDAY	SATURDAY	SUNDAY
5	**6** Lailat al-Qadr	**7**
12	**13**	**14**
19	**20**	**21**
26 Arbor Day	**27**	**28**

EXPLORE YOUR PURPOSE

That feeling of pride you have after sending in a donation to your favorite charity, helping a friend with a task or wrapping up a day of service? **A sense of purpose can linger — and positively affect your mental health.** Research published in the journal *Sociological Forum* in 2013 found that giving back just one day a month may provide a greater sense of purpose and help people feel more connected to their communities.

MARCH

M	T	W	T	F	S	S
				1	2	3
4	5	6	7	8	9	10
11	12	13	14	15	16	17
18	19	20	21	22	23	24
25	26	27	28	29	30	31

MAY

M	T	W	T	F	S	S
		1	2	3	4	5
6	7	8	9	10	11	12
13	14	15	16	17	18	19
20	21	22	23	24	25	26
27	28	29	30	31		

M	T	W	T	F	S	S
1	**2**	**3**	**4**	**5**	**6**	**7**
8	9	10	11	12	13	14
15	16	17	18	19	20	21
22	23	24	25	26	27	28
29	30					

"Try to be a rainbow in someone else's cloud."

—MAYA ANGELOU

1 MONDAY ◑ April Fools' Day

2 TUESDAY

3 WEDNESDAY

4 THURSDAY

5 FRIDAY

6 SATURDAY Lailat al-Qadr

7 SUNDAY

APRIL 8-14

2024

M	T	W	T	F	S	S
1	2	3	4	5	6	7
8	**9**	**10**	**11**	**12**	**13**	**14**
15	16	17	18	19	20	21
22	23	24	25	26	27	28
29	30					

Make Sustainable Choices

1. Ditch single-use plastics. Opt for reusable water bottles, mugs, straws, totes and produce bags. Choose recycled paper, glass or aluminum packaging.

2. Research brands. Consider the energy use and waste creation of the manufacturing process, the packaging, how the product is shipped, which communities are doing the labor and how the employees are treated.

3. Shop organic when you can. Whether the item is food, bedding, clothing or something else, organic products generally mean a smaller chemical environmental footprint.

4. Use water wisely. Case in point? Dishwashing giant Dawn created its Powerwash Dish Spray in an effort to reduce the water and energy demands associated with hand-washing dishes. It's designed to be sprayed on, eliminating the need for presoaking. A final wipe and rinse with water is all that's needed. Compared with hand-washing dishes and cookware, it offers significant water and energy savings.

8 MONDAY ●

9 TUESDAY

10 WEDNESDAY Eid al-Fitr

11 THURSDAY

12 FRIDAY

13 SATURDAY

14 SUNDAY

M	T	W	T	F	S	S
1	2	3	4	5	6	7
8	9	10	11	12	13	14
15	**16**	**17**	**18**	**19**	**20**	**21**
22	23	24	25	26	27	28
29	30					

3 Strategies for Seasonal Spiff-Ups

These are some of the no-fail tricks our pros use in their own homes to get cleaning and reorganizing jobs done most efficiently.

1. Focus your efforts. No time (or energy) for a top-to-bottom scrubdown? Prioritize one, two or a few major chores that need the most attention and that, once done, will bring you the biggest sense of accomplishment. Smaller tasks can wait.

2. Make it manageable. Break big jobs into weekend, daily, even hourly chunks according to the time you have available. Whether you wash all the windows or just one, when time's up, you'll have crossed a vital task off your list.

3. Limit distractions. It's easy to get sidetracked and thrown off course. To stay focused, turn off social media, tune in to music or a podcast and let family know it's "do not disturb" until you're done.

15 MONDAY ◑ Tax Day

16 TUESDAY

17 WEDNESDAY

18 THURSDAY

19 FRIDAY

20 SATURDAY

21 SUNDAY

APRIL 22-28
2024

M	T	W	T	F	S	S
1	2	3	4	5	6	7
8	9	10	11	12	13	14
15	16	17	18	19	20	21
22	**23**	**24**	**25**	**26**	**27**	**28**
29	30					

Pick the Best Rain Boots

Wet shoes are uncomfortable, so a reliable pair of good rain boots is essential to having fun when wet weather rolls around. However, because rain boots are specifically made to keep feet dry, their fully enclosed design can certainly create a hassle when it's time to slip them on and off. You've no doubt noticed that very few effective rain boots have laces or zippers, because those would create openings through which water could seep.

If you're fed up with a cumbersome pair, try shorter boots with tabs at the openings or ones with easy-to-pull features. Footwear brand Bogs carries unique rain boots for men, women and kids with wide built-in handles that are strategically placed to allow for easy maneuvering without sacrificing efficacy. Regardless, make sure your rain boots are made with fully waterproof materials (like rubber) and have deep treads on the bottom for traction.

22 **MONDAY** Passover Begins
Earth Day

23 **TUESDAY** ○

24 **WEDNESDAY**

25 **THURSDAY**

26 **FRIDAY**

27 **SATURDAY**

28 **SUNDAY**

MAY 2024

MONDAY	TUESDAY	WEDNESDAY	THURSDAY
		1 May Day ◑	**2**
6	**7** ●	**8**	**9**
13	**14**	**15** ◑	**16**
20	**21**	**22**	**23** ○
27 Memorial Day	**28**	**29**	**30** ◑

FRIDAY	SATURDAY	SUNDAY
3	**4**	**5** Cinco de Mayo
10	**11**	**12** Mother's Day
17	**18** Armed Forces Day	**19**
24	**25**	**26**
31		

Feel Good Goal

FOCUS ON SMALL GOALS

If your sweeping resolutions (Slash sugar! Organize your entire closet!) never stick, here's a thought for you: Are you biting off more than you can chew? **Smaller, more attainable goals add up to create a big impact**, according to the health experts. Break down the biggest items on your wish list and focus on tackling those instead. Want to walk 10,000 steps a day? Start with a goal of half that for a month and then increase to 7,500.

APRIL						
M	T	W	T	F	S	S
1	2	3	4	5	6	7
8	9	10	11	12	13	14
15	16	17	18	19	20	21
22	23	24	25	26	27	28
29	30					

JUNE						
M	T	W	T	F	S	S
					1	2
3	4	5	6	7	8	9
10	11	12	13	14	15	16
17	18	19	20	21	22	23
24	25	26	27	28	29	30

APRIL 29–MAY 5

2024

M	T	W	T	F	S	S
29	30	1	2	3	4	5
6	7	8	9	10	11	12
13	14	15	16	17	18	19
20	21	22	23	24	25	26
27	28	29	30	31		

"Limit your ALWAYS and your NEVERS."

–AMY POEHLER

29 MONDAY

30 TUESDAY

1 WEDNESDAY ◑ May Day

2 THURSDAY

3 FRIDAY

4 SATURDAY

5 SUNDAY Cinco de Mayo

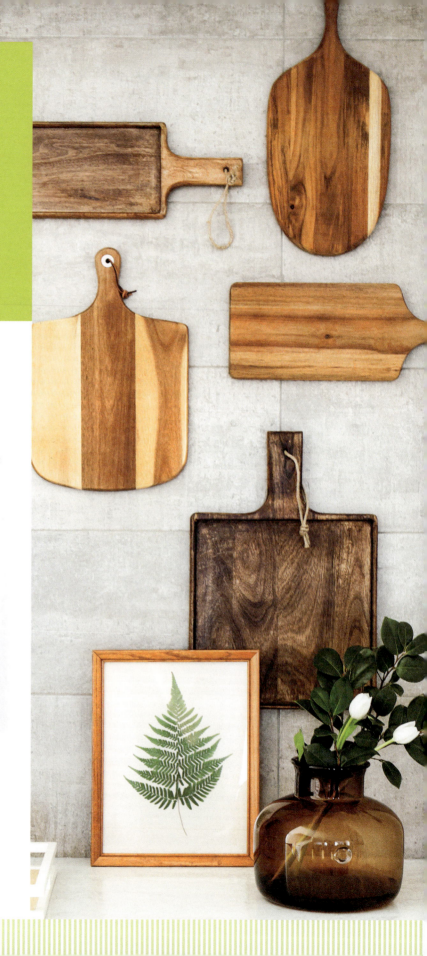

MAY 6-12
2024

M	T	W	T	F	S	S
		1	2	3	4	5
6	7	8	9	10	11	12
13	14	15	16	17	18	19
20	21	22	23	24	25	26
27	28	29	30	31		

Display Your Kitchen Gear

Add some flair to the heart of the home by filling a blank wall with an array of beautiful kitchen items such as wooden cutting boards, copper pots or vintage spoons. Mix and match different shapes, sizes and colors for an arrangement that suits your space and your taste. Katie Rioux, founder of DWK Interiors, who designed the display at right, recommends using Command strips for easy hanging. "This kind of collection is a great way to add personality to the space," she says.

Consider, too, how you might also free up valuable storage areas by displaying large or frequently used items within easy reach. It's a handy way to showcase favorite items in your collection AND make them more accessible for daily use.

TRY THIS TO FEEL
ORGANIZED
Take advantage of high shelves. *Cabinets above the refrigerator and other hard-to-reach (but great to have) storage areas are perfect for items that you access less often.*

6 MONDAY

7 TUESDAY ●

8 WEDNESDAY

9 THURSDAY

10 FRIDAY

11 SATURDAY

12 SUNDAY Mother's Day

MAY 13–19
2024

M	T	W	T	F	S	S
		1	2	3	4	5
6	7	8	9	10	11	12
13	14	15	16	17	18	19
20	21	22	23	24	25	26
27	28	29	30	31		

Master Eye Makeup

Follow this handy visual reference: Apply a single or base eyeshadow shade all over the lid; for depth, add a darker color to the crease. Glide eyeliner along the upper lashline, plus the outer V, waterline and lower lashline for more impact if desired. Dot highlighter (or cover-up one to two shades lighter than skin) onto inner corner and brow-bone to brighten eyes.

Want to make your eyes even more visually stunning? The classic Hollywood makeup pro secret for illuminating eyes by lining them with white eyeliner has gotten a modern upgrade: Rather than using white, which can be harsh, swipe a beige eyeliner along your lower waterline.

And if your work gets smudged along the way, there's no need to take it all off and start from scratch. Instead of wiping it with your finger, which can worsen the smudge, dip a cotton swab or a small make-up brush in a liquid makeup remover, then dab it directly on the spot to remove just the errant color.

13 MONDAY

14 TUESDAY

15 WEDNESDAY ☽

16 THURSDAY

17 FRIDAY

18 SATURDAY Armed Forces Day

19 SUNDAY

MAY 20-26
2024

M	T	W	T	F	S	S
		1	2	3	4	5
6	7	8	9	10	11	12
13	14	15	16	17	18	19
20	**21**	**22**	**23**	**24**	**25**	**26**
27	28	29	30	31		

Three Cheers for Chives

Part of the allium family, this zesty, tender herb offers subtle onion-garlic flavor that's perfect for spring dishes. Here's one of our Test Kitchen's favorite ways to use it:

CHERRY TOMATO DRESSING

Active **10 min.** | Total **10 min.**

- 1 small shallot (thinly sliced)
- ⅓ cup 1-in. pieces chives
- ¼ cup each basil and parsley (roughly chopped)
- 1 lb cherry or grape tomatoes (quartered)
- ¾ cup oil
- ¼ cup red wine vinegar
- ½ tsp each kosher salt and pepper

To large mason jar, add the shallot, chives, basil, parsley, half the tomatoes, oil, vinegar, and salt and pepper; shake vigorously. Add remaining tomatoes and shake. Spoon over cooked steak, fish or chicken.

SERVES 8 About 200 cal, 21 g fat (1.5 g sat fat), 1 g pro, 125 mg sodium, 3 g carb, 1 g fiber

20 MONDAY

21 TUESDAY

22 WEDNESDAY

23 THURSDAY ○

24 FRIDAY

25 SATURDAY

26 SUNDAY

JUNE 2024

MONDAY	TUESDAY	WEDNESDAY	THURSDAY
3	4	5	6 ●
10	11	12	13
17	18	19 Juneteenth	20 First Day of Summer
24	25	26	27

FRIDAY	SATURDAY	SUNDAY
	1	**2**
7	**8**	**9**
14 Flag Day ◑	**15**	**16** Father's Day
21 ○	**22**	**23**
28 ◐	**29**	**30**

REASSESS YOUR STRESS

The problem is not that we have stress (it's inevitable), it's the way both your mind and body react to these minor daily stressors that truly matters. **Consider what message stress is sending you.** Take some time to do a quick inventory of the stressors you regularly encounter and the impact on your life. For example, it might be telling you that you need to develop boundaries or that you're taking on too high of a workload. Explore how to use this insight to make changes that help alleviate some of those chronic daily stressors.

MAY						
M	**T**	**W**	**T**	**F**	**S**	**S**
		1	2	3	4	5
6	7	8	9	10	11	12
13	14	15	16	17	18	19
20	21	22	23	24	25	26
27	28	29	30	31		

JULY						
M	**T**	**W**	**T**	**F**	**S**	**S**
1	2	3	4	5	6	7
8	9	10	11	12	13	14
15	16	17	18	19	20	21
22	23	24	25	26	27	28
29	30	31				

**MAY 27–
JUNE 2**

2024

M	T	W	T	F	S	S
27	28	29	30	31	1	2
3	4	5	6	7	8	9
10	11	12	13	14	15	16
17	18	19	20	21	22	23
24	25	26	27	28	29	30

"A flower blossoms for its own joy."

—OSCAR WILDE

27 MONDAY Memorial Day

28 TUESDAY

29 WEDNESDAY

30 THURSDAY ◑

31 FRIDAY

1 SATURDAY

2 SUNDAY

JUNE 3-9

2024

M	T	W	T	F	S	S
					1	2
3	4	5	6	7	8	9
10	11	12	13	14	15	16
17	18	19	20	21	22	23
24	25	26	27	28	29	30

Paint "Inside the Box"

Transform a subdued bookshelf into a fun focal point with a pop of bold color. Coordinate with the room's furnishings for a cohesive look, as Judy Pickett of Design Lines Signature did in this vibrant entryway, and keep decor to a minimum. "Stick with a muted palette for the objects on the shelves so they don't distract from the color," Pickett advises.

When picking paint colors, don't rely on the little square swatches to make a final decision: Once on the wall, paint can look very different than it does on the sample card. Colors often look brighter once on the wall, and the light in your room can have a dramatic impact on the way the color reads. Pick a few finalists, then purchase sample cans to decide which color you like best.

TRY THIS TO FEEL
CALM

Treat yourself to fresh blooms and pamper your senses.

There's nothing like walking into a room and seeing a fresh bouquet. Instead of waiting for a special occasion or someone else to buy them for you, pick up an arrangement today.

3 MONDAY

4 TUESDAY

5 WEDNESDAY

6 THURSDAY ●

7 FRIDAY

8 SATURDAY

9 SUNDAY

JUNE 10-16
2024

M	T	W	T	F	S	S
					1	2
3	4	5	6	7	8	9
10	11	12	13	14	15	16
17	18	19	20	21	22	23
24	25	26	27	28	29	30

Conquer the Cosmetic Clutter

Beyond the obvious signs—dried mascara or separated foundation—it can be tough to tell when your makeup is past its prime. U.S. labeling regulations don't require an expiration date on cosmetics, though some have an open jar symbol on their packaging that indicates how many months the product will perform at peak quality.

When in doubt, follow our expert advice on how often to make over your makeup bag.

- Mascara and liquid eyeliner: **Every season**
- Skincare products, sunscreens and liquid foundation: **Every six months**
- Hair products (except hairspray): **Every year**
- Powder-based cosmetics, lipsticks and nail polishes: **Every two years**

10 MONDAY

11 TUESDAY

12 WEDNESDAY

13 THURSDAY

14 FRIDAY ☽ Flag Day

15 SATURDAY

16 SUNDAY Father's Day

JUNE 17-23

2024

M	T	W	T	F	S	S
				1	2	
3	4	5	6	7	8	9
10	11	12	13	14	15	16
17	18	19	20	21	22	23
24	25	26	27	28	29	30

Wow-Worthy Windows

Nothing says spring like sparkling glass and dust-free surfaces. You can see clearly now!

POLISH AND BUFF. Spritz windowpanes and door panes with enough cleaner to dissolve grime. Wipe with a clean, wet sponge to remove dirt. Buff with a clean, dry microfiber cloth, first vertically and then horizontally to zap streaks.

FRESHEN CURTAINS AND DRAPES. For an instant upgrade, vacuum panels and valances with your machine's upholstery attachment to remove dust. Then go over them with a garment steamer to revive their look and get rid of odors. If it's time for a deeper clean, remove window treatments and head to your local dry cleaner: It's a little more cumbersome and costly, but you'll love the results, and it will save you the work of washing and ironing them.

17 MONDAY

18 TUESDAY

19 WEDNESDAY Juneteenth

20 THURSDAY First Day of Summer

21 FRIDAY ○

22 SATURDAY

23 SUNDAY

JUNE 24-30
2024

M	T	W	T	F	S	S
				1	2	
3	4	5	6	7	8	9
10	11	12	13	14	15	16
17	18	19	20	21	22	23
24	25	26	27	28	29	30

Eat More Beans

You know beans are a smart meat alternative, but it can be easy to fall into a "chili, burrito, chili" culinary rut. Below, some beans-piration: three delicious ways to reap these pulses' protein, fiber and antioxidant goodness.

MAKE CRUNCHY BEAN CROUTONS (SHOWN). Dawn Jackson Blatner, R.D.N., author of *The Superfood Swap*, suggests this: Toss 1 can rinsed chickpeas with 1 Tbsp olive oil and seasonings; roast at 400°F for 40 min. (shake every 10 min.)—and voilà! a crunchy, protein-rich snack!

HACK YOUR MEAT. Replace half of your burger meat with mashed pinto beans, or make chickpeas and lentils the stars of your next Taco Tuesday or Meatball Monday.

BUILD A LUNCH BOWL. Use bean-based rice as your base (buy on Amazon or search online to find popular brands available near you). Top with plenty of veggies, a drizzle of your favorite dressing or even another protein.

24 MONDAY

25 TUESDAY

26 WEDNESDAY

27 THURSDAY

28 FRIDAY ◑

29 SATURDAY

30 SUNDAY

Your Guide to a Splendid
SUMMER

Explore the great outdoors this season! Whether that's time at the beach, in a forest, or in your own backyard, make lasting memories with Mother Nature.

ARRANGE AN OUTDOOR
Living Wall

Freshen up your patio by mounting potted plants to a blank wall. For easy hanging, drill a hole in one side of each of several terra-cotta pots with a bit slightly larger than the screws you're using (if the pot doesn't have a drainage hole in the bottom, drill one there as well).

Fill the pots with low-maintenance cascading plants or herbs that can thrive in sun and shade, pick a wall you can see easily from an outdoor seating area and affix the pots to it with mortar screws. "We wanted to make this wall visually interesting," says designer Tori Rubinson, who handled the project above. Mission accomplished!

Prepare the Perfect Patio

Outdoor spaces need care too. Make sure yours is always guest-ready with these simple steps.

STASH CUSHIONS. The best way to keep removable chair cushions and throw pillows (like the one above from World Market) clean is to shelter them from dirt and dampness after use and during the off-season. Invest in a waterproof deck box for easy access when you need them and easy storage when you don't.

SPOT-CLEAN FURNITURE. Thoroughly cleaning chairs and tables at the start and end of your outdoor season is key, but regular touch-ups are what keep them ready for impromptu get-togethers. Store a stash of heavy-duty cleaning wipes, like Clorox Multi-Purpose Paper Towel Wipes, nearby to remove dirt and stains quickly without having to rinse.

BRIGHTEN BRICK. Stone, brick and concrete walks and accents are prone to getting dirty and stained when exposed to the elements. Use a cleaner like Granite Gold Outdoor Stone Cleaner. Gentle and safe around plants, it comes in a size that attaches to your garden hose for extra pressure and reach.

PAINT GRAPHIC "TILES"

Transform your outdoor space by swapping out an ordinary rug for DIY painted "tiles" in a bold pattern. Laura Gummerman of A Beautiful Mess, a DIY crafts and food brand, enlivened a basic concrete patio floor with a black-and-white paint design that resembles triangular tiles. The trick to recreating the budget-friendly look: "Clean the concrete well, use a concrete primer before painting your pattern and add a layer of clear matte sealer to extend the paint's wear time," she says.

GO GREEN
Warm up a black-and-white palette with plants to "make it feel lush and cozy," says Laura Gummerman of A Beautiful Mess.

USE YOUR YARD AS A PLAYGROUND

Is it even summer without a few outdoor games? Invite loved ones to enjoy some friendly competition with a round of ring toss, cornhole or dice—but don't skimp on decor. Pepper in items like lanterns and a chic woven chair that will come in handy for quick breaks when the games heat up. For a memorable summer bash, here are some things to keep in mind:

PLAN AHEAD. Lay out plates, accessories and decorative items the day before the party so you won't have to hurry to arrange it all right before your guests arrive.

MAKE EASY DISHES. Prepare apps and sides—a caprese platter, crunchy coleslaw, potato salad—hours ahead of an event. Grilled meat is a go-to main course, but you can also cook brisket or a batch of roasted chicken legs the day before.

PUMP UP THE PRETTY. Amp up decor with fun pillows, seat cushions and assorted planters filled with herbs, flowers and even small veggie plants.

Make Your Own Veggie Burger

ROASTED EGGPLANT VEGGIE BURGER

Active **40 min.** | Total **1 hr.**

If the idea of a processed frozen vegetable burger doesn't whet your appetite, this hearty recipe is a real game changer.

- 1 12-oz eggplant, halved lengthwise
- 3 Tbsp olive oil, divided Kosher salt and pepper
- 1 medium onion, chopped
- 2 cloves garlic, chopped
- 1 Tbsp paprika
- 1 tsp dried thyme
- 1 tsp dried oregano
- ½ cup quick-cooking oats
- ½ cup raw walnuts
- 1 15-oz can lentils, rinsed
- 1 large egg yolk
- 1 tsp Worcestershire sauce
- 4 slices American cheese (optional)
- 4 brioche buns
  Iceberg or romaine lettuce, mayonnaise, tomato, red onion and pickled jalapeño, for topping

1. Heat oven to 375°F. Line rimmed baking sheet with nonstick baking mat or parchment.

2. Score flesh side of each eggplant half in diamond pattern. Brush cut sides with 1 Tbsp oil and season with ¼ tsp salt. Roast until very tender, 25 to 30 min.

3. Meanwhile, heat remaining 2 Tbsp oil in medium skillet on medium. Add onion, season with ½ tsp each salt and pepper and cook, covered, stirring occasionally, 5 min.

4. Stir in garlic, paprika, thyme and oregano and cook, stirring, 2 min. Let cool.

5. In food processor, pulse oats and walnuts until very finely chopped; transfer mixture to small bowl.

6. Scoop eggplant into food processor, discarding skin. Add lentils, egg yolk, Worcestershire sauce and onion mixture and process until nearly smooth. Add walnut-oat mixture and pulse to combine.

7. Divide eggplant mixture in 4 and scoop onto prepared pan, then gently shape mixture into round patties. Bake until browned, 10 to 13 min., adding cheese during last minute of cooking if using. Let cool 5 min. before making sandwiches with buns and toppings.

SERVES 4 About 515 cal, 24 g fat (4 g sat), 18 g pro, 796 mg sodium, 61 g carb, 15 g fiber

MAKE HAND-DYED NAPKINS

Bring color to any table with watercolor napkins. Once you soak napkins in water and wring out the excess, brush fabric paint in small strokes from bottom to top, diluting the paint with water as you work your way up. Hang and let dry completely before adding them to your place settings.

JULY 2024

MONDAY	TUESDAY	WEDNESDAY	THURSDAY
1	2	3	4 Independence Day
8	9	10	11
15	16	17	18
22	23	24	25
29	30	31	

FRIDAY	SATURDAY	SUNDAY
5 ●	**6**	**7**
12	**13** ◑	**14**
19	**20**	**21** ○
26	**27** ◐	**28**

Feel Good Goal

STAY COMFORTABLE

Summer clothing is full of fashion options, but **what you wear should help you feel good both inside and out.** Take time to add a few new pieces to your wardrobe (and ditch anything ill-fitting, worn or unflattering). Stumped for ideas? Breezy, lightweight dresses are a good bet. A loose silhouette is forgiving *and* evokes carefree appeal. But the best part? They can be worn with white sneakers for day, as a beach cover-up with comfy flip-flops, or fancied up with cute wedges for a special occasion.

JUNE						
M	T	W	T	F	S	S
					1	2
3	4	5	6	7	8	9
10	11	12	13	14	15	16
17	18	19	20	21	22	23
24	25	26	27	28	29	30

AUGUST						
M	T	W	T	F	S	S
			1	2	3	4
5	6	7	8	9	10	11
12	13	14	15	16	17	18
19	20	21	22	23	24	25
26	27	28	29	30	31	

JULY 1–7

2024

M	T	W	T	F	S	S
1	2	3	4	5	6	7
8	9	10	11	12	13	14
15	16	17	18	19	20	21
22	23	24	25	26	27	28
29	30	31				

"The cure for anything is salt water: sweat, tears, or the sea."

—ISAK DINESEN

1 MONDAY

2 TUESDAY

3 WEDNESDAY

4 THURSDAY Independence Day

5 FRIDAY ●

6 SATURDAY

7 SUNDAY

JULY 8–14
2024

M	T	W	T	F	S	S
1	2	3	4	5	6	7
8	**9**	**10**	**11**	**12**	**13**	**14**
15	16	17	18	19	20	21
22	23	24	25	26	27	28
29	30	31				

Breathe Like a Yogi

Women tend to put their own needs on the back burner, but even just a few minutes of "me time" will help you reboot. Pausing to take a few deep breaths enables you to relax—and it benefits your heart as well. In fact, one study found that choosing to be alone for even 15 minutes could lead to more relaxation and less stress.

But if you want to take it a step further, studies also suggest that 20 minutes of specialized yoga breathing can lift your mood and even improve your memory. Try this alternate-nostril technique: Make an L with your right thumb and first finger; take a deep breath; press the right side of your nose with your thumb to block your right nostril; exhale; inhale through your left nostril; block your left nostril and release the right; exhale; inhale. Switch sides; repeat.

TRY THIS TO FEEL
CALM

Give your eyes a break. *Prevent digital eyestrain by following the rule of 20: Every 20 minutes, take a 20-second break to look at something 20 feet away.*

8 MONDAY

9 TUESDAY

10 WEDNESDAY

11 THURSDAY

12 FRIDAY

13 SATURDAY ◐

14 SUNDAY

JULY 15–21
2024

M	T	W	T	F	S	S
1	2	3	4	5	6	7
8	9	10	11	12	13	14
15	**16**	**17**	**18**	**19**	**20**	**21**
22	23	24	25	26	27	28
29	30	31				

Try a Grill Basket

Outdoor cooking is always a great strategy for avoiding a hot and steamy kitchen in the summer, and the truth is that you can prepare far more foods on your grill if you use a handy grill basket. Here are our best tips for success:

To help prevent foods from sticking, and for extra browning, preheat your basket on the grill before adding ingredients.

Toss ingredients—we like snap peas, green beans, small potatoes and carrots—with oil and seasonings before placing in the grill basket.

Arrange foods in a single layer to maximize browning and minimize steaming. Foods can cook more quickly on a grill, so work in batches if necessary.

Resist the urge to flip or stir your food often. As with cooking indoors, the less you turn it, the more flavor and browning you'll develop.

TRY THIS TO FEEL
ORGANIZED
Make sure you have all your grill supplies handy before you start. Even just a portable table can help you create an impromptu outdoor kitchen station near your grill.

15 MONDAY

16 TUESDAY

17 WEDNESDAY

18 THURSDAY

19 FRIDAY

20 SATURDAY

21 SUNDAY ○

JULY 22–28
2024

M	T	W	T	F	S	S
1	2	3	4	5	6	7
8	9	10	11	12	13	14
15	16	17	18	19	20	21
22	23	24	25	26	27	28
29	30	31				

3 No-Fail Strategies for Summer Makeup

GO FOR SHEER SHADES. "Rich, deep colors have their place, but they can look heavy in summer," explains Troy Surratt, a makeup artist in New York City and cofounder of Surratt Beauty. To lighten up your look, switch to sheer versions of your go-to lip and eye colors. Bonus: Because translucent shades are subtler, you almost can't go overboard.

GET HELP FOR SHINE. To eliminate oil and sweat in seconds, nothing beats blotting papers. "They're cheap and easy—you just press and go," says Ashunta Sheriff-Kendricks, a celebrity makeup artist in New York City. If you also need to perk up your makeup, blot first, then follow up with a pressed powder.

SEAL IT WITH SETTING SPRAY. For insurance that your makeup will last all day (and all night) in heat, spritz on a makeup setting spray to lock in your look. It's a go-to move professional makeup artists use to keep celebrities' makeup intact under hot lights.

22 MONDAY

23 TUESDAY

24 WEDNESDAY

25 THURSDAY

26 FRIDAY

27 SATURDAY ◐

28 SUNDAY

AUGUST 2024

MONDAY	TUESDAY	WEDNESDAY	THURSDAY
			1
5	6	7	8
12	◑ 13	14	15
19	○ 20	21	22
26	◑ 27	28	29

FRIDAY	SATURDAY	SUNDAY
2	**3**	**4** ●
9	**10**	**11**
16	**17**	**18**
23	**24**	**25**
30	**31**	

Feel
Good
Goal

BE ONE WITH NATURE

When people connect with nature, they tend to have a greater sense of well-being, happiness and even higher levels of personal growth. **Make a point to spend more time outdoors this month**, reconnecting with a favorite pastime:

- Take your lunch break outside
- Walk in the park or find a nearby trail
- Visit a botanical garden if trails and parks are inaccessible
- Join a community garden
- Try walking barefoot to really connect with nature

JULY						
M	T	W	T	F	S	S
1	2	3	4	5	6	7
8	9	10	11	12	13	14
15	16	17	18	19	20	21
22	23	24	25	26	27	28
29	30	31				

SEPTEMBER						
M	T	W	T	F	S	S
						1
2	3	4	5	6	7	8
9	10	11	12	13	14	15
16	17	18	19	20	21	22
23	24	25	26	27	28	29
30						

"When all else fails, take a vacation."

–BETTY WILLIAMS

29 MONDAY

30 TUESDAY

31 WEDNESDAY

1 THURSDAY

2 FRIDAY

3 SATURDAY

4 SUNDAY ●

AUGUST 5-11
2024

M	T	W	T	F	S	S
			1	2	3	4
5	6	7	8	9	10	11
12	13	14	15	16	17	18
19	20	21	22	23	24	25
26	27	28	29	30	31	

Make Your Beach Walk Rock

It's hard to believe that something as enjoyable as feeling a warm breeze while you take in the gorgeous shoreline is actually good for you — but it is! Here's what to keep in mind:

BE STRATEGIC. When it's breezy, start your workout by walking against the wind so your energy will be highest for the hardest part. Then, on your return trip, the wind will be at your back, giving you a little push to the finish line.

CHECK THE TIDE SCHEDULE. If you walk two miles one way while the tide is coming in, you might be left with just a sliver of sand on the way back.

BE PREPARED. This means bringing water to drink and, of course, sunscreen. "It can be cloudy and breezy, but that sun can still get you," says Michele Stanten, an ACE-certified fitness instructor, a walking coach and the author of *Walk Your Way to Better Health*. To lessen your UV exposure, take sunrise or sunset walks.

5 MONDAY

6 TUESDAY

7 WEDNESDAY

8 THURSDAY

9 FRIDAY

10 SATURDAY

11 SUNDAY

AUGUST 12–18
2024
....

M	T	W	T	F	S	S
			1	2	3	4
5	6	7	8	9	10	11
12	**13**	**14**	**15**	**16**	**17**	**18**
19	20	21	22	23	24	25
26	27	28	29	30	31	

Tips for Stress-Free Flying

AIM TO TRAVEL LATE MORNING OR EARLY AFTERNOON . . .
If possible, avoid choosing early morning or late-night departure times for flights, trains or buses. Instead aim to travel between 11 a.m. and 4 p.m. local time. That way, you won't be forced to scramble during rush hour. This window of time is usually the least busy at most airports and often offers the cheapest ticket prices, too, so you save your sanity and your cash.

. . . AND NEVER (EVER!) BOOK THE FIRST OR LAST FLIGHT OF THE DAY. When weather is bad or when an airline needs to make unexpected changes to its schedule, it will often target the first or last flights of the day for a change. If you must take a super-early flight, consider booking a room at the airport so at least you're super close. Take note: Many travel sites do super-cheap last-minute airport bookings.

12 MONDAY ◐

13 TUESDAY

14 WEDNESDAY

15 THURSDAY

16 FRIDAY

17 SATURDAY

18 SUNDAY

AUGUST 19–25
2024

M	T	W	T	F	S	S
			1	2	3	4
5	6	7	8	9	10	11
12	13	14	15	16	17	18
19	**20**	**21**	**22**	**23**	**24**	**25**
26	27	28	29	30	31	

Make Your Own Ice Cream

Here's a super simple way to use up summer fruits before they go bad. An added bonus? No ice cream maker required!

EASIEST-EVER FRUIT ICE CREAM

Active **10 min.** | Total **10 min. plus freezing**

- 2 lbs frozen fruit
- ½ cup sweetened condensed milk (7 oz)
- 1 Tbsp honey
- ½ teaspoon kosher salt

1. In food processor, pulse fruit, occasionally scraping side of bowl, until finely chopped and fluffy. Add sweetened condensed milk, honey and salt; pulse, occasionally scraping side of bowl, until smooth and whirring around blade in continuous wave.
2. Transfer mixture to 5- by 9-in. loaf pan. Freeze, uncovered, until set, about 4 hours. Serve or cover tightly with plastic wrap and freeze up to 2 weeks.

FROZEN FRUIT GUIDE

2 lbs strawberries = 7 cups
SERVES 5 About 175 cal, 2.5 g fat (1.5 g sat fat), 3 g pro, 225 mg sodium, 36 g carb, 4 g fiber

2 lbs blueberries = 8 cups
SERVES 5 About 200 cal, 3.5 g fat (1.5 g sat fat), 3 g pro, 225 mg sodium, 42 g carb, 5 g fiber

2 lbs mango chunks = 7 cups
SERVES 5 About 220 cal, 3 g fat (1.5 g sat fat), 4 g pro, 225 mg sodium, 47 g carb, 3 g fiber

19 MONDAY ○

20 TUESDAY

21 WEDNESDAY

22 THURSDAY

23 FRIDAY

24 SATURDAY

25 SUNDAY

SEPTEMBER 2024

MONDAY	TUESDAY	WEDNESDAY	THURSDAY
2 Labor Day ●	3	4	5
9	10	11 ◑	12
16	17 ○	18	19
23	24 ◐	25	26
30			

FRIDAY	SATURDAY	SUNDAY
		1
6	**7**	**8**
13	**14**	**15**
20	**21**	**22** First Day of Fall
27	**28**	**29**

EAT HEALTHIER

Cooking can be a fun and useful hobby, and September is the best time of year for an abundance of fresh produce, so this month **find your inner chef.** Sign up for a cooking class or commit to cooking a few meals a week using a new ingredient. Whatever your comfort level in the kitchen happens to be, regularly cooking for yourself is a great way to discover new flavors and techniques, and enjoy the fruits of your labor, too. Want to get started tonight? Look toward healthy cookbooks for inspiration or try some of our favorite nutritious dinner recipes at goodhousekeeping.com/dinner-recipes.

AUGUST

M	T	W	T	F	S	S
			1	2	3	4
5	6	7	8	9	10	11
12	13	14	15	16	17	18
19	20	21	22	23	24	25
26	27	28	29	30	31	

OCTOBER

M	T	W	T	F	S	S
	1	2	3	4	5	6
7	8	9	10	11	12	13
14	15	16	17	18	19	20
21	22	23	24	25	26	27
28	29	30	31			

AUGUST 26–SEPTEMBER 1

2024

M	T	W	T	F	S	S
26	27	28	29	30	31	1
2	3	4	5	6	7	8
9	10	11	12	13	14	15
16	17	18	19	20	21	22
23	24	25	26	27	28	29
30						

"All dreams are within reach. All you have to do is keep moving towards them."

–VIOLA DAVIS

26 MONDAY ◑

27 TUESDAY

28 WEDNESDAY

29 THURSDAY

30 FRIDAY

31 SATURDAY

1 SUNDAY

SEPTEMBER 2-8
2024

M	T	W	T	F	S	S
						1
2	3	4	5	6	7	8
9	10	11	12	13	14	15
16	17	18	19	20	21	22
23	24	25	26	27	28	29
30						

Enjoy the Taste of Summer

If your garden has produced a bumper crop of basil, go ahead and make a double batch of this easy pesto. Freeze in ice cube trays, then pop into a freezer-safe container for up to 3 months.

ONE-STEP CLASSIC PESTO

Active **10 min.** | Total **10 min.**

- 3 cups fresh basil leaves
- 1/3 cup grated Parmesan
- 1/4 cup pine nuts, toasted
- 2 tsp grated lemon zest plus 2 tsp lemon juice
- 1 clove garlic, grated
- 1/2 tsp kosher salt
- 1/2 cup extra virgin olive oil

In food processor, pulse the basil, Parmesan, pine nuts, lemon zest plus juice, garlic and salt. With the machine running, slowly add the oil.

MAKES 1 CUP About 85 cal (per tbsp), 9 g fat (1 g sat fat), 1 g pro, 90 mg sodium, 1 g carb, 0 g fiber

TRY THIS TO FEEL
HAPPY

Homemade pesto makes a great gift. Load extra pesto into a small glass jar, top with a thin layer of olive oil, cover and refrigerate until you're ready to share the love.

2 MONDAY ● Labor Day

3 TUESDAY

4 WEDNESDAY

5 THURSDAY

6 FRIDAY

7 SATURDAY

8 SUNDAY

SEPTEMBER 9–15
2024

M	T	W	T	F	S	S
						1
2	3	4	5	6	7	8
9	10	11	12	13	14	15
16	17	18	19	20	21	22
23	24	25	26	27	28	29
30						

Plant Your Fall Garden Now

Even though most flowers bloom during the spring months, that doesn't mean that your fall garden has to be left behind. Now is the time to get planting, and here's what to consider getting in the ground.

LETTUCE. With good soil, lettuce can thrive during the autumn season. This fast-growing vegetable, especially baby lettuce, can be ready to harvest in just about 30 days from sowing.

RADISHES. Perfect for containers or garden beds, radishes can grow in as little as 20 days. Just be sure to keep the soil moist and be mindful of proper spacing (one inch apart for seeds and 12 inches between rows).

CALENDULA. These vibrant yellow and orange flowers, whose petals can be used in salads, prefer partial shade as well as fertile, well-drained soil. Typically, they grow up to two feet tall.

9 MONDAY

10 TUESDAY

11 WEDNESDAY ◑

12 THURSDAY

13 FRIDAY

14 SATURDAY

15 SUNDAY

SEPTEMBER 16–22

2024

M	T	W	T	F	S	S
						1
2	3	4	5	6	7	8
9	10	11	12	13	14	15
16	17	18	19	20	21	22
23	24	25	26	27	28	29
30						

Love Your Leftovers

If you have some extra chicken or steak leftover from a grill night, here are three easy ways to enjoy an extra meal (or two)!

TACOS. Cut in small pieces, warm and toss with a bit of chili powder, then wrap in tortillas with an easy slaw.

PITA POCKETS. Slice cold and stuff into a pita with quick-pickled dill cucumbers and feta.

RICE BOWLS. Quickly sauté it with your favorite sauce, serve over rice and sprinkle with scallions and sesame seeds.

TRY THIS TO FEEL
ORGANIZED

Keep a Sharpie and some labels in a drawer by the fridge. Make it a habit to mark the date on your leftovers — it's the best way to avoid food that has been lingering a little too long.

16 MONDAY

17 TUESDAY ○

18 WEDNESDAY

19 THURSDAY

20 FRIDAY

21 SATURDAY

22 SUNDAY First Day of Fall

SEPTEMBER 23–29
2024

M	T	W	T	F	S	S
						1
2	3	4	5	6	7	8
9	10	11	12	13	14	15
16	17	18	19	20	21	22
23	24	25	26	27	28	29
30						

Make Your Own Sauce

Making your own sauce lets you adjust it for your taste—you might even end up with a signature sauce! Try adding a little oomph with a few chili peppers, 2 cloves garlic, pressed, or a half tablespoon grated fresh ginger to the mix. Finish with sesame seeds and a squeeze of fresh lime juice (if desired).

CLASSIC TERIYAKI SAUCE

Active **5 min.** | Total **20 min.**

- ½ cup sake
- ½ cup mirin
- ½ cup reduced-sodium soy sauce
- 1 Tbsp sugar

1. In small saucepan, combine sake, mirin, sauce and sugar. Simmer, stirring occasionally, until sugar has dissolved, 3 to 5 min.

2. Continue simmering gently until mixture has thickened slightly and coats back of spoon, 12 to 15 min. more.

MAKES 1 CUP About 20 cal (per tbsp), 0 g fat (0 g sat fat), 1 g pro, 290 mg sodium, 4 g carb, 0 g fiber

23 MONDAY

24 TUESDAY ◑

25 WEDNESDAY

26 THURSDAY

27 FRIDAY

28 SATURDAY

29 SUNDAY

Inspiring Ways to Relax This

FALL

Sweater weather is here! Get ready to enjoy cooler weather and all the favorite holiday traditions that await this season.

TRICKS FOR
Good Gift Giving

Few things are as gratifying as seeing someone's face light up when they open the perfect gift. However, a looming birthday and an empty shopping cart can be anxiety-inducing. Save yourself the stress and turn shopping into a year-round activity: When you see an appropriate item, just buy it, even if you give it later.

Here's some more helpful advice to consider from Hollywood's top gift guru, Lash Fary, author of *Fabulous Gifts*.

TRUST YOUR GUT. "If you see an item that reminds you of your wife or your best friend, pay attention," says Fary. "Nothing is better than when a person opens a gift and says, 'This is so me!'"

PUT CARE INTO HOW A PRESENT LOOKS. "Presentation is at least half of your gift," says Fary. "You don't have to be the most amazing wrapper. Just take the time to do it." For best results, add some ribbon or a fresh flower.

USE YOUR WORDS. "Never underestimate the power of a note," says Fary. "The more you can say something sentimental or make the person feel something, the more value it adds to the gift."

Design Your Bedroom for the Ultimate R&R

Looking to warm up your own personal retreat? There's nothing quite like coming home after a long day and cozying up in your own haven-like bedroom. And that's exactly why so many designers make efforts to integrate coziness into even the chicest of bedrooms. Whether it be by way of plush throw pillows or a fuzzy rug, designers are all about piling on the luxe layers.

Regardless of whether you're looking to improve your sleep quality, design a comfortable place to WFH or cue up a legitimate hibernation den, the coziness factor of a bedroom can be leveled up in a few fundamental ways. Talk to any home decor expert and they'll tell you that lighting will always be key. Turn off your overhead fixture and opt instead for a pair of bedside lamps, or strategically install a pendant light to create a relaxing ambiance. If you're blessed enough to have a bedroom with plenty of natural light, thank the design deities and utilize it!

Of course, the star of any bedroom is—you guessed it—the bed. Employing a stately bed with warm wood tones will create comfort, while a dramatic canopy bed will make your beauty sleep feel even more luxurious. Just as important are the things that layer on top of your bed. A feather-soft duvet, cashmere blanket and plush pillows will all make your bedroom a snug sanctuary.

SET A MOOD WITH SCENT

"Instead of a candle, use an essential oil diffuser to create a specific vibe in your space," says GH Senior Home Editor Monique Valeris. To relax, try lavender, chamomile or eucalyptus oil. For more focus and energy, peppermint or grapefruit works well. If you need a diffuser, try one from Vitruvi Stone, a GH Institute Lab favorite.

Bake the Perfect Treat

SALTED CARAMEL COOKIES

Active **1 hr. 20 min.** | Total **2 hr. 15 min.**

Studded with chocolate chips and filled with chewy caramels,
these cookies are sure to become a year-round favorite.

2 cups all-purpose flour
1⅓ cups unsweetened cocoa powder
2 tsp baking soda
¼ tsp kosher salt
1 cup (2 sticks) unsalted butter, at room temp
½ cup granulated sugar
1½ cups packed light brown sugar
2 large eggs, at room temp
2 tsp pure vanilla extract
¼ cup buttermilk
12 oz bittersweet chocolate, coarsely chopped (about 2 cups)
36 soft caramels
Flaky sea salt, for topping

1. Line baking sheet with parchment paper. In medium bowl, sift together flour, cocoa powder, baking soda and kosher salt, then whisk to combine; set aside.

2. In large bowl, using electric mixer, beat butter and sugars on medium speed until light and fluffy, about 3 min. Reduce mixer speed to low and mix in eggs 1 at a time, then add vanilla.

3. Add flour mixture in 2 parts, alternating with buttermilk and beating just until incorporated.

4. Fold in chocolate chunks by hand, then refrigerate at least 30 min.

5. Scoop dough into balls (2 Tbsp each) and place on prepared sheet; refrigerate while preparing caramels. With back of spoon, flatten each caramel into ¾-in.-wide disk. Flatten each ball of cookie dough into disk and wrap around flattened caramel; return to baking sheet and refrigerate.

6. Heat oven to 350°F. Line 2 baking sheets with parchment paper and arrange chilled cookies on sheets, spacing 2 in. apart. Sprinkle with flaky sea salt and bake, rotating positions of pans halfway through, until set around edges, 10 to 12 min. Let cool on sheets 5 min. Transfer to wire rack to cool completely.

MAKES 36 COOKIES About 230 cal (per cookie), 11.5 g fat (7 g sat fat), 2 g pro, 255 mg sodium, 30 g carb, 2 g fiber

MAKE TIME FOR A COOKIE SWAP

Cookie swaps are fabulous for discovering new favorite recipes (especially since they've been vetted by your loved ones)! And there's something very satisfying about sharing your creations with the people you love.

For best results, request that partygoers print out their recipes from the Internet or photocopy their original handwritten or cookbook recipes. An even easier option: Take photos of the recipes at the party and email them to your guests later.

To help keep your stress levels low, have these three rules in mind when selecting your perfect batch.

1 It's smart to use recipes that you've made (and loved!) before or that come from a source you truly trust. The yummiest desserts are often the simplest, so don't hesitate to make Grandma's classic recipe.

2 Stick with recipes that have large yields (between 6 to 8 dozen cookies) or double/triple your usual go-to bake. While this may seem like a lot, remember that it's much easier to make multiple batches of the same cookie than to hunt around for the perfect mix.

3 Avoid delicate cookies that may break or crumble during the swap. Also avoid treats that can't sit out for long periods — they're not worth your (or your guests') time.

OCTOBER 2024

MONDAY	TUESDAY	WEDNESDAY	THURSDAY
	1	**2** ●	**3** Rosh Hashanah
7	**8**	**9**	**10** ☽
14 Indigenous Peoples' Day	**15**	**16**	**17** ○
21	**22**	**23**	**24** ☾
28	**29**	**30**	**31** Halloween Diwali

FRIDAY	SATURDAY	SUNDAY
4	5	6
11	12 Yom Kippur Begins	13
18	19	20
25	26	27

EXPRESS YOURSELF

Sketch. Paint. Knit. **Do something this month to get your creative juices flowing.** Creative arts have an extraordinary capacity to elevate and transcend our negative emotional experiences through self-expression, as well as to connect us more deeply and authentically with others. That's because the process of self-expression allows you to step out of your own experience and draw from a larger perspective.

SEPTEMBER

M	T	W	T	F	S	S
						1
2	3	4	5	6	7	8
9	10	11	12	13	14	15
16	17	18	19	20	21	22
23	24	25	26	27	28	29
30						

NOVEMBER

M	T	W	T	F	S	S
				1	2	3
4	5	6	7	8	9	10
11	12	13	14	15	16	17
18	19	20	21	22	23	24
25	26	27	28	29	30	

SEPTEMBER 30–OCTOBER 6

2024

M	T	W	T	F	S	S
30	1	2	3	4	5	6
7	8	9	10	11	12	13
14	15	16	17	18	19	20
21	22	23	24	25	26	27
28	29	30	31			

"One loyal friend is worth ten thousand relatives."

– EURIPIDES

30 MONDAY

1 TUESDAY

2 WEDNESDAY ●

3 THURSDAY Rosh Hashanah

4 FRIDAY

5 SATURDAY

6 SUNDAY

OCTOBER 7-13
2024

M	T	W	T	F	S	S
	1	2	3	4	5	6
7	8	9	10	11	12	13
14	15	16	17	18	19	20
21	22	23	24	25	26	27
28	29	30	31			

Make a Delicious Breakfast

In less than 15 minutes you can dress up your plain toast with this citrus creation and set your day on the right course.

HONEY-BROILED ORANGE TOAST

Active **10 min.** | Total **15 min.**

- 2 oranges (blood orange and tangerine)
  Olive oil
- 1 Tbsp honey
- ½ cup ricotta
- 4 slices toast
  Grated lemon zest
  Cracked pepper and flaked sea salt

Remove peel and pith from the oranges and cut into ¼ in. thick slices; arrange on baking sheet rubbed with olive oil. Drizzle with honey and broil until beginning to char, 4 to 8 min. Meanwhile, whip ricotta in mini food processor. Spread on 4 thick slices of toast. Top with broiled oranges, grated lemon zest, cracked pepper and flaked salt.

SERVES 4 About 215 cal, 6 g fat (3 g sat), 9 g pro, 320 mg sodium, 32 g carb, 4 g fiber

7 MONDAY

8 TUESDAY

9 WEDNESDAY

10 THURSDAY ◑

11 FRIDAY

12 SATURDAY Yom Kippur Begins

13 SUNDAY

OCTOBER 14-20

2024

M	T	W	T	F	S	S
	1	2	3	4	5	6
7	8	9	10	11	12	13
14	15	16	17	18	19	20
21	22	23	24	25	26	27
28	29	30	31			

Wear a Skincare "Coat"

When it comes to hydration, not all moisturizing skincare products are created equal. According to GH Beauty Lab testing, says GH Beauty Lab Director Birnur Aral, Ph.D., "face lotions and creams are generally more hydrating than oils, serums and other formulas." And, she says, they can increase skin's moisture for hours. For maximum efficacy, look for moisturizers with glycerin and hyaluronic acid, which can help skin hold on to water better, plus ingredients that help repair the skin barrier, such as ceramides and niacinamide.

A GH beauty editor go-to trick for intensive hydration: At night, seal your moisturizer in with a thick coat of a rich oil, balm or ointment that can be applied to facial skin. Like a winter coat for your face, it functions as an occlusive, locking hydrating skincare ingredients and moisture into your skin as you sleep so you wake up softer, smoother and less parched. Also apply it when you're heading outdoors for an extended period in cold or dry weather to protect exposed skin from the elements and prevent it from becoming chapped or irritated.

14 **MONDAY** Indigenous Peoples' Day

15 **TUESDAY**

16 **WEDNESDAY**

17 **THURSDAY** ○

18 **FRIDAY**

19 **SATURDAY**

20 **SUNDAY**

OCTOBER 21-27

2024

M	T	W	T	F	S	S
	1	2	3	4	5	6
7	8	9	10	11	12	13
14	15	16	17	18	19	20
21	**22**	**23**	**24**	**25**	**26**	**27**
28	29	30	31			

Dress Up Your Candles

These DIY lace candles are just the thing you need for your haunted house-themed bash, and they're simple enough to put together in an afternoon. However, this idea can work just as easily for other holiday gatherings with any color palette you choose. Or get a jump on gift-giving season and stock up on a bunch of pillar candles — they make easy and practical presents, too.

To make, cut a length of lace and place it on a paper plate. Apply nonflammable black tempera paint to it, then roll the candle of your choice directly across the trim to pick up the pattern. It's best to let the paint dry for about an hour before lighting your candle. As an alternative, you can also apply the lace tape to the exterior of a glass holder for a similar look.

TRY THIS TO FEEL
ORGANIZED

If you don't have a dedicated space for crafts, load your supplies into a portable container (tackle boxes are great for this). Make sure to cover your work surface with newspaper for easy cleanup.

21 MONDAY

22 TUESDAY

23 WEDNESDAY

24 THURSDAY ◐

25 FRIDAY

26 SATURDAY

27 SUNDAY

NOVEMBER 2024

MONDAY	TUESDAY	WEDNESDAY	THURSDAY
4	5	6	7
11 Veterans Day	12	13	14
18	19	20	21
25	26	27	28 Thanksgiving

FRIDAY	SATURDAY	SUNDAY
1 All Saints' Day ●	**2**	**3** Daylight Savings Time Ends
8	**9** ◐	**10**
15 ○	**16**	**17**
22 ◑	**23**	**24**
29	**30**	

Feel Good Goal

EXERCISE YOUR BRAIN

Saving off cognitive decline is a hot research topic—and while data may be divided, it seems games can indeed play a role here. Researchers at Duke University studied participants' brain activity while they completed simple math problems and found that solving them feels like a reward, helping to curb negative feelings. So **take a few minutes every day to play a brain game or two**—they can help manage stress and anxiety, as well as boost happiness endorphins at the same time.

OCTOBER

M	T	W	T	F	S	S
	1	2	3	4	5	6
7	8	9	10	11	12	13
14	15	16	17	18	19	20
21	22	23	24	25	26	27
28	29	30	31			

DECEMBER

M	T	W	T	F	S	S
						1
2	3	4	5	6	7	8
9	10	11	12	13	14	15
16	17	18	19	20	21	22
23	24	25	26	27	28	29
30	31					

M	T	W	T	F	S	S
28	29	30	31	1	2	3
4	5	6	7	8	9	10
11	12	13	14	15	16	17
18	19	20	21	22	23	24
25	26	27	28	29	30	

"You do not find the happy life. You make it."

– CAMILLA EYRING KIMBALL

28 MONDAY

29 TUESDAY

30 WEDNESDAY

31 THURSDAY Halloween
Diwali

1 FRIDAY ● All Saints' Day

2 SATURDAY

3 SUNDAY Daylight Savings Time Ends

NOVEMBER 4-10
2024

M	T	W	T	F	S	S
				1	2	3
4	5	6	7	8	9	10
11	12	13	14	15	16	17
18	19	20	21	22	23	24
25	26	27	28	29	30	

Go with Gratitude

Experts say giving thanks actually increases happiness. "Gratitude is the antidote to negative emotions and taking things for granted," says Sonja Lyubomirsky, Ph.D., a professor of psychology at the University of California, Riverside, and the author of *The How of Happiness*. It makes you feel more positive, which paves the road to a happier mindset. Here are a few tips to get you started.

WRITE LETTERS. A note of thanks will boost both your and the recipient's mood and help you realize the power certain connections have in providing joy.

FALL ASLEEP HAPPY. As you drift off each night, think about three things you appreciate, such as an important person, highlights of the day or something you have to look forward to.

FOCUS ON LITTLE THINGS. We tend to get caught up in the major areas of life like work and relationships, but expressing thanks for sunshine after a rainy day or a kind person at the grocery store can easily restore a strong sense of gratitude.

4 MONDAY

5 TUESDAY

6 WEDNESDAY

7 THURSDAY

8 FRIDAY

9 SATURDAY ◑

10 SUNDAY

NOVEMBER 11–17
2024

M	T	W	T	F	S	S
				1	2	3
4	5	6	7	8	9	10
11	12	13	14	15	16	17
18	19	20	21	22	23	24
25	26	27	28	29	30	

Donate Food

With all the focus on food around this time of year, it's easy to forget how many people face hunger on a regular basis. An easy way to help: Sort through all the food you stocked up on and donate unopened shelf-stable products to your local food pantry (check the sell-by date first). Much needed: peanut butter, canned soups, beans, tuna, cans of pasta sauce and individual bags of rice. Items to avoid include any food with damaged packaging such as dented or bloated cans. A good rule of thumb is that if you wouldn't purchase the item in its present condition, don't donate it.

"The need has grown exponentially, but the opportunities to help have grown too," says Muzzy Rosenblatt, president of Bowery Residents' Committee, which serves 3,000 homeless New Yorkers every day. Go to feedingamerica. org for more info.

TRY THIS TO FEEL
HAPPY

Donate your time. Volunteering can raise self-esteem and lower loneliness. One study found that those who lent a helping hand felt less anxious about social situations than those who didn't.

11 MONDAY Veterans Day

12 TUESDAY

13 WEDNESDAY

14 THURSDAY

15 FRIDAY ○

16 SATURDAY

17 SUNDAY

NOVEMBER 18-24
2024

M	T	W	T	F	S	S
				1	2	3
4	5	6	7	8	9	10
11	12	13	14	15	16	17
18	**19**	**20**	**21**	**22**	**23**	**24**
25	26	27	28	29	30	

Start New Traditions

Hosting Thanksgiving this year? Switch up the usual routine with a few thoughtful ways for your guests to bring something truly special to the table.

CRAFT A CORNUCOPIA. Traditionally, a cornucopia was usually filled with the autumn harvest, plants and flowers, to show off that season's autumnal bounty. Make it your own by asking guests to bring objects that are meaningful to them. Place them in a cornucopia, a basket or other decorative container and use it as a meaningful centerpiece for your table.

EXCHANGE CHRISTMAS ORNAMENTS. If you celebrate Christmas, you know that Thanksgiving basically kicks off the festive season. Lean into it by asking each guest to bring an ornament to exchange. Some families even request that they be homemade or have a special meaning to the giver, so you can hang a little memento of everyone you love on your tree.

18 MONDAY

19 TUESDAY

20 WEDNESDAY

21 THURSDAY

22 FRIDAY ◑

23 SATURDAY

24 SUNDAY

DECEMBER 2024

MONDAY	TUESDAY	WEDNESDAY	THURSDAY
2	3	4	5
9	10	11	12
16	17	18	19
23	24 Christmas Eve	25 Christmas Day	26 Hanukkah Begins First Day of Kwanzaa
30 ●	31 New Year's Eve		

FRIDAY	SATURDAY	SUNDAY
		1 First Day of Advent ●
6	**7**	**8** ◑
13	**14**	**15** ○
20	**21** First Day of Winter	**22** ◐
27	**28**	**29**

FIND JOY

If your mind feels like a runaway freight train this month, **press the pause button to take a moment for yourself.** Try enjoying something visual like looking at a favorite album or putting flowers in your room; or, slowly sip on a warm beverage, light a nice-smelling candle or even don soft pajamas to feel warm and cozy. Switch gears so you can land in a balanced place to think more clearly about the situation instead of getting into the rut of emotional thinking.

NOVEMBER

M	T	W	T	F	S	S
				1	2	3
4	5	6	7	8	9	10
11	12	13	14	15	16	17
18	19	20	21	22	23	24
25	26	27	28	29	30	

JANUARY

M	T	W	T	F	S	S
		1	2	3	4	5
6	7	8	9	10	11	12
13	14	15	16	17	18	19
20	21	22	23	24	25	26
27	28	29	30	31		

M	T	W	T	F	S	S
25	26	27	28	29	30	1
2	3	4	5	6	7	8
9	10	11	12	13	14	15
16	17	18	19	20	21	22
23	24	25	26	27	28	29
30	31					

"The best way out is always through."

—ROBERT FROST

25 MONDAY

26 TUESDAY

27 WEDNESDAY

28 THURSDAY Thanksgiving

29 FRIDAY

30 SATURDAY

1 SUNDAY ● First Day of Advent

DECEMBER 2-8
2024

M	T	W	T	F	S	S
						1
2	3	4	5	6	7	8
9	10	11	12	13	14	15
16	17	18	19	20	21	22
23	24	25	26	27	28	29
30	31					

The Science of Gift Giving

Julian Givi, Ph.D., an assistant professor of marketing at West Virginia University, presents the data on presents:

THE THOUGHT COUNTS— REALLY. One of Givi's heartwarming findings: "Whenever there's a multi-giver situation, givers think that how their gift compares to others' gifts matters a great deal. But in the eyes of recipients, it doesn't matter that much. We find that people just care about being cared about."

THINK LONG-TERM. "When people are trying to decide between two types of gifts, they often choose the wrong one," says Givi. "Givers tend to focus on what makes a great gift in the moment. But the key is to take a step back and think about what's going to be good down the road."

PEOPLE LOVE A SPONTANEOUS GIFT. Don't limit gift giving to the holiday season. When there's no special occasion, expectation is removed, found Givi. Another bonus of a just-because gift: It's clear that it's voluntary, which "suggests that the giver cares about the recipient."

2 MONDAY

3 TUESDAY

4 WEDNESDAY

5 THURSDAY

6 FRIDAY

7 SATURDAY

8 SUNDAY ☽

M	T	W	T	F	S	S
						1
2	3	4	5	6	7	8
9	10	11	12	13	14	15
16	17	18	19	20	21	22
23	24	25	26	27	28	29
30	31					

Stop Managing Everything

Whether you're dealing with a group project at work or planning a family reunion, it's easy to fall into the trap of doing most of the work to ensure that the end result is perfect. But it's time to let other people pick up the slack. "We go through life as if we're responsible for every outcome we experience," says Amy Johnson, Ph.D., author of *The Little Book of Big Change.* "We fail to recognize just how much happens effortlessly. Seeing what is working through us, for us, without effort needed, is a giant relief."

If you're planning on hosting a big gathering in the near future, take a moment and make a plan to delegate some of the chores and responsibilities. Allowing others to shoulder some of the burden will lower your stress, and you may be pleasantly surprised with the outcome—even if it isn't perfect.

9 MONDAY

10 TUESDAY

11 WEDNESDAY

12 THURSDAY

13 FRIDAY

14 SATURDAY

15 SUNDAY ○

DECEMBER 16–22
2024

M	T	W	T	F	S	S
						1
2	3	4	5	6	7	8
9	10	11	12	13	14	15
16	17	18	19	20	21	22
23	24	25	26	27	28	29
30	31					

Make Easy Ornaments

Need a cozy craft night to take the edge off holiday stressors? These multi-dimensional ornaments are easy to put together with simple colored card stock and whatever embellishments you may have on hand.

To make, cut out five strips of paper: two 1¼" x 10", two 1¼" x 7," and one 1¼" x 5". Then punch a hole ¼" from the top and bottom of each strip. Stack the papers together: smallest in the middle, sandwiched by the medium strips, followed by the largest strips. Line up all of the strips on one end and thread a piece of string or wire through the holes and tie it off. Repeat this step on the other end of the strips, which you can then fan out. Add tassels or beads to the bottom of the ornament for extra sparkle.

TRY THIS TO FEEL
HAPPY

Don't forget the music! A spontaneous craft night is the perfect occasion to enjoy your favorite holiday tunes in the background.

16 MONDAY

17 TUESDAY

18 WEDNESDAY

19 THURSDAY

20 FRIDAY

21 SATURDAY First Day of Winter

22 SUNDAY ◑

DECEMBER 23-29
2024

M	T	W	T	F	S	S
						1
2	3	4	5	6	7	8
9	10	11	12	13	14	15
16	17	18	19	20	21	22
23	**24**	**25**	**26**	**27**	**28**	**29**
30	31					

Serve Sauce with a Twist

Want to introduce some new flavors to your regular holiday menu? This easy cranberry sauce is a winner.

FIG AND ROSEMARY CRANBERRY SAUCE

Active **5 min.** | Total **20 min.**

- 12 oz fresh or frozen cranberries
- 1 cup chopped dried figs
- ½ cup honey
- ½ sprig fresh rosemary

1. In medium saucepan, combine cranberries, figs, honey, rosemary and ½ cup water.

2. Bring mixture to a boil. Reduce heat and simmer, stirring occasionally, until cranberries burst and sauce has thickened, 15 to 20 min. Discard rosemary and serve warm or at room temp.

SERVES 8 About 130 cal, 0 g fat (0 g sat), 1 g pro, 5 mg sodium, 34 g carb, 3 g fiber

23 MONDAY

24 TUESDAY Christmas Eve

25 WEDNESDAY Christmas Day

26 THURSDAY Hanukkah Begins
First Day of Kwanzaa

27 FRIDAY

28 SATURDAY

29 SUNDAY

DECEMBER 30– JANUARY 5
2024–2025

M	T	W	T	F	S	S
						1
2	3	4	5	6	7	8
9	10	11	12	13	14	15
16	17	18	19	20	21	22
23	24	25	26	27	28	29
30	31	1	2	3	4	5

Take Some Down Time

In the whirlwind of the holidays — shopping for gifts, cleaning the house, preparing and cooking the meal, cleaning it all up and spending time with your guests in between — even the most extroverted among us may feel exhausted after it's all over. You're certainly not alone if you find yourself feeling overwhelmed in the midst of all the seasonal fun. Fortunately, there are a few easy strategies that may help. To maximize your energy, start the day on solid footing by taking just a few moments of alone time for yourself before it all begins. Try listening to music, writing in a journal, or simply reflecting on your intentions for the day. Carving out some quiet time to yourself provides an excellent opportunity to reflect on your intentions and goals. Plus, you'll be able to enjoy the excitement that much more.

TRY THIS TO FEEL
HAPPY

Discover a new podcast. *People shift their moods to match the tones of voice they're hearing, revealed a recent study. So why not cue up an inspiring podcast to give your morning the boost it deserves?*

30 MONDAY ●

31 TUESDAY New Year's Eve

1 WEDNESDAY New Year's Day

2 THURSDAY

3 FRIDAY

4 SATURDAY

5 SUNDAY

NOTES

Thank You

FOR PURCHASING THE GOOD HOUSEKEEPING 2024 LIVE LIFE BEAUTIFULLY PLANNER.

Discover more great products from
Good Housekeeping when you visit our store at:
Shop.GoodHousekeeping.com

PLUS, if you liked this year's planner, keep a lookout for next year's edition with all-new tips and advice to live your life beautifully!

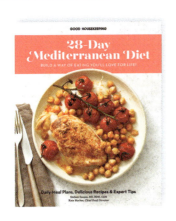

HEARST

PHOTO CREDITS

(All Left to Right/Top to Bottom)

Cover & Back Cover: ©Olivia Inman/ Stocksy United

Title page: ©Mark Scott

Copyright page: ©Panattar/ stock.adobe.com

Every Day Extraordinary: ©Daniel de la Hoz/iStock/Getty Images Plus; ©Oksana Kiian/iStock/Getty Images Plus; ©Westend61/Getty Images; ©Paul Havel; ©Becky Luigart-Stayner. Recipe and Food Stylist: Torie Cox; ©Betsie Van Der Meer/Getty Images; ©Rachel Whiting; ©Mike Garten

Winter: ©Sandy Aknine/Getty Images; ©Ol'ga Smolâk/EyeEm/Getty Images; ©Yin Yang/Getty Images; ©JGI/ Tom Grill/Getty Images; ©279photo/ stock.adobe.com; ©DeanDrobot/ iStock/Getty Images Plus; ©Poh Kim Yeoh/EyeEm/Getty Images; ©Kate Whitaker; ©Sarka Babicka/Stockfood

January 1: ©Junaid Rashid/ Getty Images

January 8: ©Raymond Forbes LLC/ Stocksy United

January 15: ©ABtop/iStock/Getty Images Plus

January 22: ©Zbynek Pospisil/iStock/ Getty Images Plus

January 29: ©Jana Akyildiz/EyeEm/ Getty Images

February 5: ©Light Field Studios/iStock/ Getty Images Plus

February 12: ©Food Collection/ Stockfood

February 19: ©Mike Garten. Prop Stylists: Lis Engelhart and Alex Mata

February 26: ©LaylaBird/Getty Images

March 4: ©Mike Garten

March 11: ©Danielle Daly. Food Stylist: Eugene Jho; Prop Stylist: Cate Geiger Kalus

March 18: ©Dan Duchars

March 25: ©Laurey Glenn

Spring: ©FollowTheFlow/iStock/Getty Images Plus; ©Ellobo1/iStock/Getty Images Plus; ©Courtesy of Amanda Walker; ©Brizmaker/iStock/Getty Images Plus; ©Cass Smith; ©Design and Photo by Lauren Macke of Home

Theology Design; ©Robert Radifera; ©Courtesy; ©iStock/Getty Images; ©Mike Garten. Food Stylist: Christine Albano; Prop Stylist: Christina Lane

April 1: ©Valeriy_G/iStock/Getty Images Plus

April 8: ©MirageC/Getty Images

April 15: ©Pavel Iarunichev/iStock/Getty Images Plus

April 22: ©Etienne_Outram/iStock/ Getty Images Plus

April 29: ©Westend61/Getty Images

May 6: ©Lindsay Nichols Photography

May 13: ©Getty Images

May 20: ©Getty Images

May 27: ©Dutch Scenery/iStock/Getty Images Plus

June 3: ©Courtesy of Design Lines Signature

June 10: ©Poba/iStock/Getty Images Plus

June 17: ©Onzeg/Getty Images

June 24: ©Mike Garten

Summer: ©Nicola Stocken; ©Photo by Stephen Karlisch. Designed by Tori Rubinson of Tori Rubinson Interiors; ©OJO_Images/Getty Images; ©Courtesy of WorldMarket.com; ©Jill Weller. Designed by Arterberry Cooke; ©Photo and Design by Laura Gummerman; ©Photo by Lauren Pressey. Designed by Linda Hayslett of LH.Designs; ©Mike Garten; ©Dimitris66/Getty Images; ©Mike Garten. Food Stylist: Simon Andrews; Prop Stylist: Alex Mata

July 1: ©Cagkansayin/iStock/Getty Images Plus

July 8: ©Jasmina007/Getty Images

July 15: ©Ekaterina Smirnova/ Getty Images

July 22: ©Puhhha/iStock/Getty Images Plus

July 29: ©Colin Anderson/Getty Images

August 5: ©KOLOstock/Getty Images

August 12: ©Richard Drury/ Getty Images

August 19: ©Mike Garten

August 26: ©EvgeniiAnd/iStock/Getty Images Plus

September 2: ©Mike Garten

September 9: ©Claudia Totir/ Getty Images

September 16: ©Mike Garten. Food Stylist: Simon Andrews; Prop Stylist: Cate Geiger Kalus

September 23: ©Mike Garten. Food Stylist: Simon Andrews; Prop Stylist: Christina Lane

Fall: ©Aksenovko/iStock/Getty Images Plus; ©Westend61/Getty Images; ©Alison Gootee; ©JLco-Julia Amaral/ iStock/Getty Images Plus; ©Petrenkod/ iStock/Getty Images Plus; ©Mark Scott. Stylist: Lorraine Dawkins; ©Ngoc Minh Ngo; ©Courtesy of Vitruvi; ©Mark Scott; ©Mike Garten. Prop and Craft Stylist: Alex Mata; ©Mike Garten. Food Stylist: Christine Albano; Prop Stylist: Raina Kattelson

September 30: ©Peter Muller/ Getty Images

October 7: ©Mike Garten. Food Stylist: Simon Andrews; Prop Stylist: Christina Lane

October 14: ©Getty Images

October 21: ©Quentin Bacon

October 28: ©FreshSplash/Getty Images

November 4: ©Nicky Lloyd/ Getty Images

November 11: ©Happy_lark/iStock/ Getty Images Plus

November 18: ©Becky Luigart-Stayner. Stylist: Anna Logan; Crafting: Sarah Scherf

November 25: ©Wbritten/Getty Images

December 2: ©Anastasiia Krivenok/ Getty Images

December 9: ©Mike Garten. Prop Stylists: Lis Engelhart and Alex Mata

December 16: ©Mike Garten. Prop and Craft Stylists: Lis Engelhart and Alex Mata

December 23: ©Mike Garten. Food Stylist: Christine Albano; Prop Stylist: Alex Mata

December 30: ©Fotostorm/iStock/Getty Images Plus